Tom Stoppard
Plays One

Tom Stoppard's other work includes: *Rosencrantz and Guildenstern Are Dead*, *Jumpers*, *Travesties*, *Night and Day*, *After Magritte*, *The Real Thing*, *Enter A Free Man*, *Hapgood*, *Arcadia*, *Indian Ink* (a stage adaptation of his own play, *In the Native State*) and *The Invention of Love*. *Arcadia* won him his sixth Evening Standard Award, The Olivier Award and the Critics Award. *Rosencrantz and Guildenstern Are Dead*, *Travesties* and *The Real Thing* won Tony Awards.

His radio plays include: *If You're Glad I'll Be Frank*, *Albert's Bridge* (Italia Prize), *Where Are They Now?*, *Artist Descending A Staircase*, *The Dog It Was That Died*, *In the Native State* (Sony Award).

Work for television includes: *Professional Foul* (Bafta Award, Broadcasting Press Guild Award). His film credits include *Rosencrantz and Guildenstern Are Dead* which he also directed (winner of the Golden Lion, Venice Film Festival).

TOM STOPPARD
Plays One

The Real Inspector Hound,
After Magritte,
Dirty Linen,
New–Found–Land,
Dogg's Hamlet and
Cahoot's Macbeth

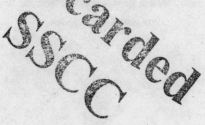

Introduced by the author

faber and faber
LONDON · BOSTON

This collection first published in 1993 as
The Real Inspector Hound and Other Entertainments
Reissued as *Tom Stoppard: Plays One* in 1996
by Faber and Faber Limited
3 Queen Square London WC1N 3AU

Photoset by Parker Typesetting Service, Leicester
Printed and bound in Great Britain by
Mackays of Chatham PLC, Chatham, Kent

A CIP record for this book is available from the British Library

ISBN 0-571-17765-4

4 6 8 10 9 7 5 3

CONTENTS

PREFACE

The earliest of these plays, *The Real Inspector Hound*, grew out of a few pages I wrote in 1960 and came back to in 1967. There were no critics in the story when I began it. Moon and Birdboot started off simply as two people in an audience, until it occurred to me that making them critics would give them something to be, and give me something to play with. As for Higgs, Moon's first-string senior, he remained an off-stage character until (well into the 1967 version) I realized that he was the perfect answer to my problem: who was the corpse under the sofa?

I mention these things because nobody quite believes the playwright's line about characters taking over a story. I never quite believe it myself. Looking back at *Hound*, I can't see the point of starting to write it if one didn't know the one thing which, more than any other, made the play worth writing: that Higgs was dead and under the sofa. When the idea came it seemed an amazing piece of luck, and I constantly remember that because my instinct, even now, is to want to know more about the unwritten play than is knowable, or good to know. So, whenever I finally set off again, knowing far too little and trusting in luck, I always gain courage from remembering the wonderful day when Moon and Birdboot led the lagging author to the discovery that – of course! – 'It's Higgs!'

After Magritte, *Dirty Linen* (incorporating *New-Found-Land*) and *Dogg's Hamlet, Cahoot's Macbeth* were all written for Ed Berman's Inter-Action company between 1972 and 1980. Circumstances have changed even more dramatically for Pavel Kohout than for Ed Berman but I have let the original Introductions stand as a marker for the spirit of the time. The Almost Free Theatre, the Fun Art Bus and the rest of them were phenomena of a decade which was simultaneously playful and desperately serious; and perhaps that still describes Berman himself, now operating from a mooring on the Embankment, on a boat which only moves up and down with the tide, but which couldn't be called mothballed while Berman is on the bridge.

Czechoslovakia is a different country now, a great joy to all concerned but not without its ironies, for while there is no longer a need for an underground Living Room Theatre, the above-ground theatre has lost the generous subsidies which came with obedience under Communism, and times are hard.

After Magritte often serves as a companion piece to *The Real Inspector Hound*, which I think is appropriate in at least one way: neither play is about anything grander than itself. A friendly critic described *Hound* as being as useful as an ivory Mickey Mouse. *After Magritte* may be slightly less useful than that. Both plays are performed more often than the other two. The 'role of the theatre' is much debated (by almost nobody, of course), but the thing defines itself in practice first and foremost as a recreation. This seems satisfactory.

TOM STOPPARD
1993

THE REAL
INSPECTOR HOUND

CHARACTERS

MOON
BIRDBOOT
MRS. DRUDGE
SIMON
FELICITY
CYNTHIA
MAGNUS
INSPECTOR HOUND

The first performance of *The Real Inspector Hound* was given on 17th June 1968, at the Criterion Theatre, London, when the cast was as follows:

MOON	Richard Briers
BIRDBOOT	Ronnie Barker
MRS. DRUDGE	Josephine Tewson
SIMON	Robin Ellis
FELICITY	Patricia Shakesby
CYNTHIA	Caroline Blakiston
MAGNUS	Antony Webb
INSPECTOR HOUND	Hugh Walters

Directed by Robert Chetwyn

Designed by Hutchinson Scott

The first thing is that the audience appear to be confronted by their own reflection in a huge mirror. Impossible. However, back there in the gloom—not at the footlights—a bank of plush seats and pale smudges of faces. (The total effect having been established, it can be progressively faded out as the play goes on, until the front row remains to remind us of the rest and then, finally, merely two seats in that row—one of which is now occupied by MOON. *Between* MOON *and the auditorium is an acting area which represents, in as realistic an idiom as possible, the drawing-room of Muldoon Manor. French windows at one side. A telephone fairly well upstage (i.e. towards* MOON). *The* BODY *of a man lies sprawled face down on the floor in front of a large settee. This settee must be of a size and design to allow it to be wheeled over the body, hiding it completely. Silence. The room. The* BODY. MOON.

MOON *stares blankly ahead. He turns his head to one side then the other, then up, then down—waiting. He picks up his programme and reads the front cover. He turns over the page and reads.*

He turns over the page and reads.

He turns over the page and reads.

He turns over the page and reads.

He looks at the back cover and reads.

He puts it down and crosses his legs and looks about. He stares front. Behind him and to one side, barely visible, a man enters and sits down: BIRDBOOT.

Pause. MOON *picks up his programme, glances at the front cover and puts it down impatiently. Pause. . . . Behind him there is the crackle of a chocolate-box, absurdly loud.* MOON *looks round. He and* BIRDBOOT *see each other. They are clearly known to each other. They acknowledge each other with constrained waves.* MOON *looks straight ahead.* BIRDBOOT *comes down to join him.*

Note: *Almost always,* MOON *and* BIRDBOOT *converse in tones suitable for an auditorium, sometimes a whisper. However good the acoustics might be, they will have to have microphones where they are sitting. The effect must be* not *of sound picked up, amplified and flung out at the audience, but of sound picked up, carried and gently dispersed around the auditorium.*

Anyway, BIRDBOOT, *with a box of Black Magic, makes his way down to join* MOON *and plumps himself down next to him, plumpish middle-aged* BIRDBOOT *and younger taller, less-relaxed* MOON.

BIRDBOOT (*sitting down; conspiratorially*): Me and the lads have had a meeting in the bar and decided it's first-class family entertainment but if it goes on beyond half-past ten it's self-indulgent—pass it on . . . (*and laughs jovially*) I'm on my own tonight, don't mind if I join you?

MOON: Hello, Birdboot.

BIRDBOOT: Where's Higgs?

MOON: I'm standing in.

MOON AND BIRDBOOT: Where's Higgs?

MOON: Every time.

BIRDBOOT: What?

MOON: It is as if we only existed one at a time, combining to achieve continuity. I keep space warm for Higgs. My presence defines his absence, his absence confirms my presence, his presence precludes mine. . . . When Higgs and I walk down this aisle together to claim our common seat, the oceans will fall into the sky and the trees will hang with fishes.

BIRDBOOT (*he has not been paying attention, looking around vaguely, now catches up*): Where's Higgs?

MOON: The very sight of me with a complimentary ticket is enough. The streets are impassable tonight, the country is rising and the cry goes up from hill to hill—Where—is— Higgs? (*Small pause.*) Perhaps he's dead at last, or trapped in a lift somewhere, or succumbed to amnesia, wandering the land with his turn-ups stuffed with ticket-stubs.

(BIRDBOOT *regards him doubtfully for a moment.*)

BIRDBOOT: Yes. . . . Yes, well I didn't bring Myrtle tonight—not exactly her cup of tea, I thought, tonight.

MOON: Over her head, you mean?

BIRDBOOT: Well, no—I mean it's a sort of a *thriller*, isn't it?

MOON: Is it?

BIRDBOOT: That's what I heard. Who killed thing?—no one will leave the house.

MOON: I suppose so. Underneath.

BIRDBOOT: *Underneath*?!? It's a whodunnit, man!—Look at it!
(*They look at it. The room. The* BODY. *Silence.*)
Has it started yet?

MOON: Yes.
(*Pause. They look at it.*)

BIRDBOOT: Are you sure?

MOON: It's a pause.

BIRDBOOT: You can't start with a *pause*! If you want my opinion there's total panic back there. (*Laughs and subsides.*) Where's Higgs tonight, then?

MOON: It will follow me to the grave and become my epitaph—Here lies Moon the second string: where's Higgs? . . . Sometimes I dream of revolution, a bloody *coup d'etat* by the second rank—troupes of actors slaughtered by their understudies, magicians sawn in half by indefatigably smiling glamour girls, cricket teams wiped out by marauding bands of twelfth men—I dream of champions chopped down by rabbit-punching sparring partners while eternal bridesmaids turn and rape the bridegrooms over the sausage rolls and parliamentary private secretaries plant bombs in the Minister's Humber—comedians die on provincial stages, robbed of their feeds by mutely triumphant stooges—
—and—march—
—an army of assistants and deputies, the seconds-in-command, the runners-up, the right-hand men— storming the palace gates wherein the second son has already mounted the throne having committed regicide with a croquet-mallet—stand-ins of the world stand up!—
(*Beat.*) Sometimes I dream of Higgs.

(*Pause.* BIRDBOOT *regards him doubtfully. He is at a loss, and grasps reality in the form of his box of chocolates.*)

BIRDBOOT (*Chewing into mike*): Have a chocolate!

MOON: What kind?

BIRDBOOT: (*Chewing into mike*): Black Magic.

MOON: No thanks.

(*Chewing stops dead.*)

(*Of such tiny victories and defeats. . . .*)

BIRDBOOT: I'll give you a tip, then. Watch the girl.

MOON: You think she did it?

BIRDBOOT: No, no—the *girl*, watch her.

MOON: What girl?

BIRDBOOT: You won't know her, I'll give you a nudge.

MOON: *You* know her, do you?

BIRDBOOT (*suspiciously, bridling*): What's *that* supposed to mean?

MOON: I beg your pardon?

BIRDBOOT: I'm trying to tip you a wink—give you a nudge as good as a tip—for God's sake, Moon, what's the matter with you? —you could do yourself some good, spotting her first time out—she's new, from the provinces, going straight to the top. I don't want to put words into your mouth but a word from us and we could make her.

MOON: I suppose you've made dozens of them, like that.

BIRDBOOT (*instantly outraged*): I'll have you know I'm a family man devoted to my homely but good-natured wife, and if you're suggesting—

MOON: No, no—

BIRDBOOT: —A man of my scrupulous morality—

MOON: I'm sorry—

BIRDBOOT: —falsely besmirched.

MOON: Is that her?

(*For* MRS. DRUDGE *has entered.*)

BIRDBOOT: —don't be absurd, wouldn't be seen dead with the old —ah.

(MRS. DRUDGE *is the char, middle-aged, turbanned. She heads straight for the radio, dusting on the trot.*)

MOON (*reading his programme*): Mrs. Drudge the Help.

RADIO (*without preamble, having been switched on by* MRS. DRUDGE):
We interrupt our programme for a special police message.
(MRS. DRUDGE *stops to listen.*)
The search still goes on for the escaped madman who is on
the run in Essex.

MRS. DRUDGE (*fear and dismay*): Essex!

RADIO: County police led by Inspector Hound have received a
report that the man has been seen in the desolate marshes
around Muldoon Manor.
(*Fearful gasp from* MRS. DRUDGE.)
The man is wearing a darkish suit with a lightish shirt. He is
of medium height and build and youngish. Anyone seeing a
man answering to this description and acting suspiciously, is
advised to phone the nearest police station.
(*A man answering this description has appeared behind* MRS.
DRUDGE. *He is acting suspiciously. He creeps in. He creeps
out.* MRS. DRUDGE *does not see him. He does not see the body.*)
That is the end of the police message.
(MRS. DRUDGE *turns off the radio and resumes her cleaning.
She does not see the body. Quite fortuitously, her view of the
body is always blocked, and when it isn't she has her back to it.
However, she is dusting and polishing her way towards it.*)

BIRDBOOT: So that's what they say about me, is it?

MOON: What?

BIRDBOOT: Oh, I know what goes on behind my back—sniggers—
slanders—hole-in-corner innuendo— What have you heard?

MOON: Nothing.

BIRDBOOT (*urbanely*): Tittle tattle. Tittle, my dear fellow, tattle.
I take no notice of it—the sly envy of scandal mongers—I
can afford to ignore them, I'm a respectable married man—

MOON: Incidentally——

BIRDBOOT: Water off a duck's back, I assure you.

MOON: Who was that lady I saw you with last night?

BIRDBOOT (*unexpectedly stung into fury*): How dare you! (*More
quietly*) How dare you. Don't you come here with your slimy
insinuations! My wife Myrtle understands perfectly well that
a man of my critical standing is obliged occasionally to

mingle with the world of the footlights, simply by way of keeping *au fait* with the latest——

MOON: I'm sorry——

BIRDBOOT: That a critic of my scrupulous integrity should be vilified and pilloried in the stocks of common gossip——

MOON: Ssssh——

BIRDBOOT: I have nothing to hide!—why, if this should reach the ears of my beloved Myrtle——

MOON: Can I have a chocolate?

BIRDBOOT: What? Oh—— (*Mollified.*) Oh yes—my dear fellow— yes, let's have a chocolate—— No point in—yes, good show. (*Pops chocolate into his mouth and chews.*) Which one do you fancy?—Cherry? Strawberry? Coffee cream? Turkish delight?

MOON: I'll have montelimar.
    (*Chewing stops.*)

BIRDBOOT: Ah. Sorry. (*Just missed that one.*)

MOON: Gooseberry fondue?

BIRDBOOT: No.

MOON: Pistacchio fudge? Nectarine cluster? Hickory nut praline? Chateau Neuf du Pape '55 cracknell?

BIRDBOOT: I'm afraid not. . . . Caramel?

MOON: Yes, all right.

BIRDBOOT: Thanks very much. (*He gives* MOON *a chocolate. Pause.*) Incidentally, old chap, I'd be grateful if you didn't mention —I mean, you know how these misunderstandings get about. . . .

MOON: What?

BIRDBOOT: The fact is, Myrtle simply doesn't *like* the theatre. . . . (*He tails off hopelessly.* MRS. DRUDGE, *whose discovery of the body has been imminent, now—by way of tidying the room— slides the couch over the corpse, hiding it completely. She resumes dusting and humming.*)

MOON: By the way, congratulations, Birdboot.

BIRDBOOT: What?

MOON: At the Theatre Royal . Your entire review reproduced in neon!

BIRDBOOT (*pleased*): Oh . . . that old thing.

MOON: You've seen it, of course.

BIRDBOOT (*vaguely*): Well, I was passing. . . .

MOON: I definitely intend to take a second look when it has settled down.

BIRDBOOT: As a matter of fact I have a few colour transparencies —I don't know whether you'd care to . . .?

MOON: Please, please—love to, love to. . . .

(BIRDBOOT *hands over a few colour slides and a battery-powered viewer which* MOON *holds up to his eyes as he speaks.*) Yes . . . yes . . . lovely . . . awfully sound. It has scale, it has colour, it is, in the best sense of the word, electric. Large as it is, it is a small masterpiece—I would go so far as to say— kinetic without being pop, and having said that, I think it must be said that here we have a review that adds a new dimension to the critical scene. I urge you to make haste to the Theatre Royal, for this is the stuff of life itself.

(*Handing back the slides, morosely*): All I ever got was "Unforgettable" on the posters for . . . What was it?

BIRDBOOT: Oh—yes—I know. . . . Was that you? I thought it was Higgs.

(*The phone rings.* MRS. DRUDGE *seems to have been waiting for it to do so and for the last few seconds has been dusting it with an intense concentration. She snatches it up.*)

MRS. DRUDGE (*into phone*): Hello, the drawing-room of Lady Muldoon's country residence one morning in early spring? . . . He*llo*!—the draw—— Who? Who did you wish to speak to? I'm afraid there is no one of that name here, this is all very mysterious and I'm sure it's leading up to something, I hope nothing is amiss for we, that is Lady Muldoon and her houseguests, are here cut off from the world, including Magnus, the wheelchair-ridden half-brother of her lady-ship's husband Lord Albert Muldoon who ten years ago went out for a walk on the cliffs and was never seen again— and all alone, for they had no children.

MOON: Derivative, of course.

BIRDBOOT: But quite sound.

MRS. DRUDGE: Should a stranger enter our midst, which I very much doubt, I will tell him you called. Good-bye.

(She puts down the phone and catches sight of the previously seen suspicious character who has now entered again, more suspiciously than ever, through the french windows. He senses her stare, freezes, and straightens up.)

SIMON: Ah!—hello there! I'm Simon Gascoyne, I hope you don't mind, the door was open so I wandered in. I'm a friend of Lady Muldoon, the lady of the house, having made her acquaintance through a mutual friend, Felicity Cunningham, shortly after moving into this neighbourhood just the other day.

MRS. DRUDGE: I'm Mrs. Drudge. I don't live in but I pop in on my bicycle when the weather allows to help in the running of charming though somewhat isolated Muldoon Manor. Judging by the time *(she glances at the clock)* you did well to get here before high water cut us off for all practical purposes from the outside world.

SIMON: I took the short cut over the cliffs and followed one of the old smugglers' paths through the treacherous swamps that surround this strangely inaccessible house.

MRS. DRUDGE: Yes, many visitors have remarked on the topographical quirk in the local strata whereby there are no roads leading from the Manor, though there *are* ways of getting *to* it, weather allowing.

SIMON: Yes, well I must say it's a lovely day so far.

MRS. DRUDGE: Ah, but now that the cuckoo-beard is in bud there'll be fog before the sun hits Foster's Ridge.

SIMON: I say, it's wonderful how you country people really know weather.

MRS. DRUDGE *(suspiciously)*: Know whether what?

SIMON *(glancing out of the window)*: Yes, it does seem to be coming on a bit foggy.

MRS. DRUDGE: The fog is very treacherous around here—it rolls off the sea without warning, shrouding the cliffs in a deadly mantle of blind man's buff.

SIMON: Yes, I've heard it said.

MRS. DRUDGE: I've known whole week-ends when Muldoon Manor, as this lovely old Queen Anne House is called, might as well have been floating on the pack ice for all the good it would have done phoning the police. It was on such a week-end as this that Lord Muldoon who had lately brought his beautiful bride back to the home of his ancestors, walked out of this house ten years ago, and his body was never found.

SIMON: Yes, indeed, poor Cynthia.

MRS. DRUDGE: His name was Albert.

SIMON: Yes indeed, poor Albert. But tell me, is Lady Muldoon about?

MRS. DRUDGE: I believe she is playing tennis on the lawn with Felicity Cunningham.

SIMON (*startled*): Felicity Cunningham?

MRS. DRUDGE: A mutual friend, I believe you said. A happy chance. I will tell them you are here.

SIMON: Well, I can't really stay as a matter of fact—please don't disturb them—I really should be off.

MRS. DRUDGE: They would be very disappointed. It is some time since we have had a four for pontoon bridge at the Manor, and I don't play cards myself.

SIMON: There is another guest, then?

MRS. DRUDGE: Major Magnus, the crippled half-brother of Lord Muldoon who turned up out of the blue from Canada just the other day, completes the house-party.

(MRS. DRUDGE *leaves on this,* SIMON *is undecided.*)

MOON (*ruminating quietly*): I think I must be waiting for Higgs to die.

BIRDBOOT: What?

MOON: Half afraid that I will vanish when he does.

(*The phone rings.* SIMON *picks it up.*)

SIMON: Hello?

MOON: I wonder if it's the same for Puckeridge?

BIRDBOOT AND SIMON (*together*): Who?

MOON: Third string.

BIRDBOOT: Your stand-in?

MOON: Does he wait for Higgs and I to write each other's
    obituary—does he dream——?

SIMON: To whom did you wish to speak?

BIRDBOOT: What's he like?

MOON: Bitter.

SIMON: There is no one of that name here.

BIRDBOOT: No—as a critic, what's Puckeridge like as a critic?

MOON (*laughs poisonously*): Nobody knows——

SIMON: You must have got the wrong number!

MOON: —there's always been me and Higgs.

> (SIMON *replaces the phone and paces nervously. Pause.*
> BIRDBOOT *consults his programme.*)

BIRDBOOT: Simon Gascoyne. It's not him, of course.

MOON: What?

BIRDBOOT: I said it's not him.

MOON: Who is it, then?

BIRDBOOT: My guess is Magnus.

MOON: In disguise, you mean?

BIRDBOOT: What?

MOON: You think he's Magnus in disguise?

BIRDBOOT: I don't think you're concentrating, Moon.

MOON: I thought you said——

BIRDBOOT: You keep chattering on about Higgs and Puckeridge
    —what's the matter with you?

MOON (*thoughtfully*): I wonder if they talk about me. . . ?

> (*A strange impulse makes* SIMON *turn on the radio.*)

RADIO: Here is another police message. Essex county police are
    still searching in vain for the madman who is at large in the
    deadly marshes of the coastal region. Inspector Hound who
    is masterminding the operation, is not available for com-
    ment but it is widely believed that he has a secret plan. . . .
    Meanwhile police and volunteers are combing the swamps
    with loud-hailers, shouting, "Don't be a madman, give
    yourself up." That is the end of the police message.

> (SIMON *turns off the radio. He is clearly nervous.* MOON *and*
> BIRDBOOT *are on separate tracks.*)

BIRDBOOT (*knowingly*): Oh yes. . . .

MOON: Yes, I should think my name is seldom off Puckeridge's lips . . . sad, really. I mean, it's no life at all, a stand-in's stand-in.

BIRDBOOT: Yes . . . yes. . . .

MOON: Higgs never gives me a second thought. I can tell by the way he nods.

BIRDBOOT: Revenge, of course.

MOON: What?

BIRDBOOT: Jealousy.

MOON: Nonsense—there's nothing *personal* in it——

BIRDBOOT: The paranoid grudge——

MOON (*sharply first, then starting to career . . .*): It is merely that it is not enough to wax at another's wane, to be held in reserve, to be on hand, on call, to step in or not at all, the substitute—the near offer—the temporary-acting—for I am Moon, continuous Moon, in my own shoes, Moon in June, April, September and no member of the human race keeps warm my bit of space—yes, I can tell by the way he nods.

BIRDBOOT: Quite mad, of course.

MOON: What?

BIRDBOOT: The answer lies out there in the swamps.

MOON: Oh.

BIRDBOOT: The skeleton in the cupboard is coming home to roost.

MOON: Oh yes. (*He clears his throat . . . for both he and* BIRDBOOT *have a "public" voice, a critic voice which they turn on for sustained pronouncements of opinion.*) Already in the opening stages we note the classic impact of the catalystic figure— the outsider—plunging through to the centre of an ordered world and setting up the disruptions—the shock waves— which unless I am much mistaken, will strip these comfortable people—these crustaceans in the rock pool of society— strip them of their shells and leave them exposed as the trembling raw meat which, at heart, is all of us. But there is more to it than that——

BIRDBOOT: I agree—keep your eye on Magnus.

(*A tennis ball bounces through the french windows, closely*

followed by FELICITY, *who is in her 20's. She wears a pretty
tennis outfit, and carries a racket.*)

FELICITY (*calling behind her*): Out!

(*It takes her a moment to notice* SIMON *who is standing
shiftily to one side.* MOON *is stirred by a memory.*)

MOON: I say, Birdboot. . . .

BIRDBOOT: That's the one.

FELICITY (*catching sight of* SIMON): You!

(FELICITY'*s manner at the moment is one of great surprise but
some pleasure.*)

SIMON (*nervously*): Er, yes—hello again.

FELICITY: What are you doing here?

SIMON: Well, I. . . .

MOON: She's——

BIRDBOOT: Sssh. . . .

SIMON: No doubt you're surprised to see me.

FELICITY: Honestly, darling, you really are extraordinary.

SIMON: Yes, well, here I am.

FELICITY: You must have been desperate to see me—I mean, I'm
flattered, but couldn't it wait till I got back?

SIMON (*bravely*): There is something you don't know.

FELICITY: What is it?

SIMON: Look, about the things I said—it may be that I got
carried away a little—we both did——

FELICITY (*stiffly*): What are you trying to say?

SIMON: I love another!

FELICITY: I see.

SIMON: I didn't make any promises—I merely——

FELICITY: You don't have to say any more——

SIMON: Oh, I didn't want to hurt you——

FELICITY: Of all the nerve!

SIMON: Well, I——

FELICITY: You philandering coward——

SIMON: Let me explain——

FELICITY: This is hardly the time and place—you think you can
barge in anywhere, whatever I happen to be doing——

SIMON: But I want you to know that my admiration for you is

sincere—I don't want you to think that I didn't mean those
things I said——

FELICITY: I'll kill you for this, Simon Gascoyne!

(*She leaves in tears, passing* MRS. DRUDGE *who has entered in
time to overhear her last remark.*)

MOON: It was her.

BIRDBOOT: I told you—straight to the top——

MOON: No, no——

BIRDBOOT: Sssh. . . .

SIMON (*to* MRS. DRUDGE): Yes, what is it?

MRS. DRUDGE: I have come to set up the card table, sir.

SIMON: I don't think I can stay.

MRS. DRUDGE: Oh, Lady Muldoon *will* be disappointed.

SIMON: Does she know I'm here?

MRS. DRUDGE: Oh yes, sir, I just told her and it put her in quite
a tizzy.

SIMON: Really? . . . Well, I suppose now that I've cleared the
air. . . . Quite a tizzy, you say . . . really . . . really. . .

(*He and* MRS. DRUDGE *start setting up for card game.* MRS.
DRUDGE *leaves when this is done.*)

MOON: Felicity!—she's the one.

BIRDBOOT: Nonsense—red herring.

MOON: I mean, it was *her!*

BIRDBOOT (*exasperated*): *What* was?

MOON: That lady I saw you with last night!

BIRDBOOT (*inhales with fury*): Are you suggesting that a man of
my scrupulous integrity would trade his pen for a mess of
potage?! Simply because in the course of my profession I
happen to have struck up an acquaintance—to have, that
is, a warm regard, if you like, for a fellow toiler in the vine-
yard of greasepaint—I find it simply intolerable to be
pillified and villoried——

MOON: I never implied——

BIRDBOOT: —to find myself the object of uninformed malice,
the petty slanders of little men——

MOON: I'm sorry——

BIRDBOOT: —to suggest that my good opinion in a journal of

unimpeachable integrity is at the disposal of the first coquette
who gives me what I want——

MOON: Sssssh——

BIRDBOOT: A ladies' man! . . . Why, Myrtle and I have been
together now for—Christ!—who's *that*?

(*Enter* LADY CYNTHIA MULDOON *through french windows. A
beautiful woman in her thirties. She wears a cocktail dress, is
formally coiffured, and carries a tennis racket.*)

(*Her effect on* BIRDBOOT *is also impressive. He half rises and
sinks back agape.*)

CYNTHIA (*entering*): Simon!

(*A dramatic freeze between her and* SIMON.)

MOON: Lady Muldoon.

BIRDBOOT: No, I mean—who *is* she?

SIMON (*coming forward*): Cynthia!

CYNTHIA: Don't say anything for a moment—just hold me.

(*He seizes her and glues his lips to hers, as they say. While
their lips are glued*——)

BIRDBOOT: She's *beautiful*—a vision of eternal grace, a poem. . .

MOON: I think she's got her mouth open.

(CYNTHIA *breaks away dramatically.*)

CYNTHIA: We can't go on meeting like this!

SIMON: We have nothing to be ashamed of!

CYNTHIA: But darling, this is madness!

SIMON: Yes!—I am mad with love for you!

CYNTHIA: Please—remember where we are!

SIMON: Cynthia, I love you!

CYNTHIA: Don't—I love Albert!

SIMON: He's dead! (*Shaking her.*) Do you understand me—
Albert's dead!

CYNTHIA: No—I'll never give up hope! Let me go! We are not
free!

SIMON: I don't care, we were meant for each other—had we but
met in time.

CYNTHIA: You're a cad, Simon! You will use me and cast me
aside as you have cast aside so many others.

SIMON: No, Cynthia!—you can make me a better person!

CYNTHIA: You're ruthless—so strong, so cruel——
  (*Ruthlessly he kisses her.*)

MOON: The son she never had, now projected in this handsome
  stranger and transformed into lover—youth, vigour, the
  animal, the athlete as aesthete—breaking down the barriers
  at the deepest level of desire.

BIRDBOOT: By jove, I think you're right. Her mouth *is* open.
  (CYNTHIA *breaks away.* MRS. DRUDGE *has entered.*)

CYNTHIA. Stop—can't you see you're making a fool of yourself!

SIMON: I'll kill anyone who comes between us!

CYNTHIA: Yes, what is it, Mrs. Drudge?

MRS. DRUDGE: Should I close the windows, my lady? The fog is
  beginning to roll off the sea like a deadly——

CYNTHIA: Yes, you'd better. It looks as if we're in for one of
  those days. Are the cards ready?

MRS. DRUDGE: Yes, my lady.

CYNTHIA: Would you tell Miss Cunningham we are waiting.

MRS. DRUDGE: Yes, my lady.

CYNTHIA: And fetch the Major down.

MRS. DRUDGE: I think I hear him coming downstairs now (*as she
  leaves*).
  (*She does: the sound of a wheelchair approaching down several
  flights of stairs with landings in between. It arrives bearing*
  MAGNUS *at about 15 m.p.h., knocking* SIMON *over violently.*)

CYNTHIA: Simon!

MAGNUS (*roaring*): Never had a chance! Ran under the wheels!

CYNTHIA: Darling, are you all right?

MAGNUS: I have witnesses!

CYNTHIA: Oh, Simon—say something!

SIMON (*sitting up suddenly*): I'm most frightfully sorry.

MAGNUS (*shouting yet*): How long have you been a pedestrian?

SIMON: Ever since I could walk.

CYNTHIA: Can you walk now. . . ?
  (SIMON *rises and walks.*)
  Thank God! Magnus, this is Simon Gascoyne.

MAGNUS: What's he doing here?

CYNTHIA: He just turned up.

MAGNUS: Really? How do you like it here?

SIMON (*to* CYNTHIA): I could stay for ever.

(FELICITY *enters.*)

FELICITY: So—you're still here.

CYNTHIA: Of course he's still here. We're going to play cards.
There's no need to introduce you two, is there, for I recall
now that you, Simon, met me through Felicity, our mutual
friend.

FELICITY: Yes, Simon is an old friend, though not as old as you,
Cynthia dear.

SIMON: Yes, I haven't seen Felicity since——

FELICITY: Last night.

CYNTHIA: Indeed? Well, you deal, Felicity. Simon, you help me
with the sofa. Will you partner Felicity, Magnus, against
Simon and me?

MAGNUS (*aside*): Will Simon and you always be partnered against
me, Cynthia?

CYNTHIA: What do you mean, Magnus?

MAGNUS: You are a damned attractive woman, Cynthia.

CYNTHIA: Please! Please! Remember Albert!

MAGNUS: Albert's dead, Cynthia—and you are still young. I'm
sure he would have wished that you and I——

CYNTHIA: No, Magnus, this is not to be!

MAGNUS: It's Gascoyne, isn't it? I'll kill him if he comes between
us!

CYNTHIA (*calling*): Simon!

(*The sofa is shoved towards the card table, once more revealing
the corpse, though not to the players.*)

BIRDBOOT: Simon's for the chop all right.

CYNTHIA: Right! Who starts?

MAGNUS: I do. No bid.

CYNTHIA: Did I hear you say you saw Felicity last night, Simon?

SIMON: Did I?—Ah yes, yes, quite—your turn, Felicity.

FELICITY: I've had my turn, haven't I, Simon?—now, it seems, it's
Cynthia's turn.

CYNTHIA: That's my trick, Felicity dear.

FELICITY: Hell hath no fury like a woman scorned, Simon.

SIMON: Yes, I've heard it said.

FELICITY: So I hope you have not been cheating, Simon.

SIMON (*standing up and throwing down his cards*): No, Felicity, it's just that I hold the cards!

CYNTHIA: Well done, Simon!

(MAGNUS *pays* SIMON, *while* CYNTHIA *deals*)

FELICITY: Strange how Simon appeared in the neighbourhood from nowhere. We know so little about him.

SIMON: It doesn't always pay to show your hand!

CYNTHIA: Right! Simon, it's your opening on the minor bid. (SIMON *plays.*)

CYNTHIA: Hm, let's see. . . . (*Plays.*)

FELICITY: I hear there's a dangerous madman on the loose.

CYNTHIA: Simon?

SIMON: Yes—yes—sorry. (*Plays.*)

CYNTHIA: I meld.

FELICITY: Yes—personally, I think he's been hiding out in the deserted cottage (*plays*) on the cliffs.

SIMON: Flush!

CYNTHIA: No! Simon—your luck's in tonight!

FELICITY: We shall see—the night is not over yet, Simon Gascoyne! (*She exits.*)

MAGNUS *pays* SIMON *again.*

SIMON (*to* MAGNUS): So you're the crippled half-brother of Lord Muldoon who turned up out of the blue from Canada just the other day, are you? It's taken you a long time to get here. What did you do—walk? Oh, I say, I'm most frightfully sorry!

MAGNUS: Care for a spin round the rose garden, Cynthia?

CYNTHIA: No, Magnus, I must talk to Simon.

SIMON: My round, I think, Major.

MAGNUS: You think so?

SIMON: Yes, Major—I do.

MAGNUS. There's an old Canadian proverb handed down from the Bladfoot Indians, which says: He who laughs last laughs longest.

SIMON: Yes, I've heard it said.

(SIMON *turns away to* CYNTHIA)

MAGNUS: Well, I think I'll go and oil my gun. (*He exits.*)

CYNTHIA: I think Magnus suspects something. And Felicity . . . Simon, was there anything between you and Felicity?

SIMON: No, no—it's over between her and me, Cynthia—it was a mere passing fleeting thing we had—but now that I have found you——

CYNTHIA: If I find that you have been untrue to me—if I find that you have falsely seduced me from my dear husband Albert —I will kill you, Simon Gascoyne!

(MRS. DRUDGE *has entered silently to witness this. On this tableau, pregnant with significance, the act ends, the body still undiscovered. Perfunctory applause.*)

(MOON *and* BIRDFOOT *seem to be completely preoccupied, becoming audible, as it were.*)

MOON: Camps it around the Old Vic in his opera cloak and passes me the tat.

BIRDBOOT: Do you believe in love at first sight?

MOON: It's not that I think I'm a better critic——

BIRDBOOT: I feel my whole life changing——

MOON: I am but it's not that.

BIRDBOOT: Oh, the world will laugh at me, I know. . . .

MOON: It is not that they are much in the way of shoes to step into. . . .

BIRDBOOT: . . . call me an infatuated old fool. . . .

MOON :. . . They are not.

BIRDBOOT: . . . condemn me. . . .

MOON: He is standing in my light, that is all.

BIRDBOOT: . . . betrayer of my class . . .

MOON: . . . an almost continuous eclipse, interrupted by the phenomenon of moonlight.

BIRDBOOT: I don't care, I'm a gonner.

MOON: And I dream. . . .

BIRDBOOT: The Blue Angel all over again.

MOON: . . . of the day his temperature climbs through the top of his head. . . .

BIRDBOOT: Ah, the sweet madness of love . . .

MOON: . . . of the spasm on the stairs. . . .

BIRDBOOT: Myrtle, farewell . . .

MOON: . . . dreaming of the stair he'll never reach——

BIRDBOOT: . . . for I only live but once. . . .

MOON: Sometimes I dream that I've killed him.

BIRDBOOT: What?

MOON: What?

(*They pull themselves together.*)

BIRDBOOT: Yes . . . yes. . . . A beautiful performance, a collector's piece. I shall say so.

MOON: A very promising debut. I'll put in a good word.

BIRDBOOT: It would be as hypocritical of me to withhold praise on grounds of personal feelings, as to withhold censure.

MOON: You're right. Courageous.

BIRDBOOT: Oh, I know what people will say—— There goes Birdboot buttering up his latest——

MOON: Ignore them——

BIRDBOOT: But I rise above that—— The fact is I genuinely believe her performance to be one of the summits in the range of contemporary theatre.

MOON: Trim-buttocked, that's the word for her.

BIRDBOOT:—the radiance, the inner sadness——

MOON: Does she actually come across with it?

BIRDBOOT: The part as written is a mere cypher but she manages to make Cynthia a real person——

MOON: *Cynthia?*

BIRDBOOT: And should she, as a result, care to meet me over a drink, simply by way of er—thanking me, as it were——

MOON: Well, you fickle old bastard!

BIRDBOOT (*aggressively*): Are you suggesting . . . ?

(BIRDBOOT *shudders to a halt and clears his throat.*)

BIRDBOOT: Well now—shaping up quite nicely, wouldn't you say?

MOON: Oh yes, yes. A nice trichotomy of forces. One must reserve judgement of course, until the confrontation, but I think it's pretty clear where we're heading.

BIRDBOOT: I agree. It's Magnus a mile off.

(*Small pause.*)

MOON: What's Magnus a mile off?

BIRDBOOT: If we knew that we wouldn't be here.

MOON (*clears throat*): Let me at once say that it has *élan* while at
the same time avoiding *éclat*. Having said that, and I think
it must be said, I am bound to ask—does this play know
where it is going?

BIRDBOOT: Well, it seems open and shut to me, Moon—Magnus
is not what he pretends to be and he's got his next victim
marked down——

MOON: Does it, I repeat, declare its affiliations? There are
moments, and I would not begrudge it this, when the play,
if we can call it that, and I think on balance we can, aligns
itself uncompromisingly on the side of life. *Je suis*, it seems
to be saying, *ergo sum*. But is that enough? I think we are
entitled to ask. For what in fact is this play concerned with?
It is my belief that here we are concerned with what I have
referred to elsewhere as the nature of identity. I think we
are entitled to ask—and here one is irresistibly reminded of
Voltaire's cry, "*Voila!*"—I think we are entitled to ask—
Where is God?

BIRDBOOT (*stunned*): Who?

MOON: Go-od.

BIRDBOOT (*peeping furtively into his programme*): God?

MOON: I think we are entitled to ask.

(*The phone rings.*)

(*The set re-illumines to reveal* CYNTHIA, FELICITY *and*
MAGNUS *about to take coffee, which is being taken round by*
MRS. DRUDGE. SIMON *is missing. The body lies in position.*)

MRS. DRUDGE (*into phone*): The same, half an hour later?...
No, I'm sorry—there's no one of that name here. (*She
replaces phone and goes round with coffee. To* CYNTHIA):
Black or white, my lady?

CYNTHIA: White please.

(MRS. DRUDGE *pours.*)

MRS. DRUDGE (*to* FELICITY): Black or white, miss?

FELICITY: White please.

(MRS. DRUDGE *pours.*)

MRS. DRUDGE (*to* MAGNUS): Black or white, Major?

MAGNUS: White please.

> (*Ditto.*)

MRS. DRUDGE (*to* CYNTHIA): Sugar, my lady?

CYNTHIA: Yes please.

> (*Puts sugar in.*)

MRS. DRUDGE (*to* FELICITY): Sugar, miss?

FELICITY: Yes please.

> (*Ditto.*)

MRS. DRUDGE (*to* MAGNUS): Sugar, Major?

MAGNUS: Yes please.

> (*Ditto.*)

MRS. DRUDGE (*to* CYNTHIA): Biscuit, my lady?

CYNTHIA: No thank you.

BIRDBOOT (*writing elaborately in his notebook*): The second act, however, fails to fulfil the promise. . . .

FELICITY: If you ask me, there's something funny going on.

> (MRS. DRUDGE's *approach to* FELICITY *makes* FELICITY *jump to her feet in impatience. She goes to the radio while* MAGNUS *declines his biscuit, and* MRS. DRUDGE *leaves.*)

RADIO: We interrupt our programme for a special police message. The search for the dangerous madman who is on the loose in Essex has now narrowed to the immediate vicinity of Muldoon Manor. Police are hampered by the deadly swamps and the fog, but believe that the madman spent last night in a deserted cottage on the cliffs. The public is advised to stick together and make sure none of their number is missing. That is the end of the police message.

> (FELICITY *turns off the radio nervously. Pause.*)

CYNTHIA: Where's Simon?

FELICITY: Who?

CYNTHIA: Simon. Have you seen him?

FELICITY: No.

CYNTHIA: Have you, Magnus?

MAGNUS: No.

CYNTHIA: Oh.

FELICITY: Yes, there's something foreboding in the air, it is as if one of *us*——

CYNTHIA: Oh, Felicity, the house is locked up tight—no one can get in—and the police are practically on the doorstep.

FELICITY: I don't know—it's just a feeling.

CYNTHIA: It's only the fog.

MAGNUS: Hound will never get through on a day like this.

CYNTHIA (*shouting at him*): *Fog!*

FELICITY: He means the Inspector.

CYNTHIA: Is he bringing a dog?

FELICITY: Not that I know of.

MAGNUS: —never get through the swamps. Yes, I'm afraid the madman can show his hand in safety now.

(*A mournful baying hooting is heard in the distance, scary.*)

CYNTHIA: What's that?!

FELICITY (*tensely*): It sounded like the cry of a gigantic hound!

MAGNUS: Poor devil!

CYNTHIA: Sssssh!

(*They listen. The sound is repeated, nearer.*)

FELICITY: There it is again!

CYNTHIA: It's coming this way—it's right outside the house!

(MRS. DRUDGE *enters.*)

MRS. DRUDGE: Inspector Hound!

CYNTHIA: A *police* dog?

(*Enter* INSPECTOR HOUND. *On his feet are his swamp boots. These are two inflatable—and inflated—pontoons with flat bottoms about two feet across. He carries a foghorn.*)

HOUND: Lady Muldoon?

CYNTHIA: Yes.

HOUND: I came as soon as I could. Where shall I put my foghorn and my swamp boots?

CYNTHIA: Mrs. Drudge will take them out. Be prepared, as the Force's motto has it, eh, Inspector? How very resourceful!

HOUND (*divesting himself of boots and foghorn*): It takes more than a bit of weather to keep a policeman from his duty.

(MRS. DRUDGE *leaves with chattels. A pause.*)

CYNTHIA: Oh—er, Inspector Hound—Felicity Cunningham, Major Magnus Muldoon.

HOUND: Good evening.

(*He and* CYNTHIA *continue to look expectantly at each other.*)

CYNTHIA AND HOUND (*together*): Well?—Sorry——

CYNTHIA: No, do go on.

HOUND: Thank you. Well, tell me about it in your own words—
take your time, begin at the beginning and don't leave
anything out.

CYNTHIA: I beg your pardon?

HOUND: Fear nothing. You are in safe hands now. I hope you
haven't touched anything.

CYNTHIA: I'm afraid I don't understand.

HOUND: I'm Inspector Hound.

CYNTHIA: Yes.

HOUND: Well, what's it all about?

CYNTHIA: I really have no idea.

HOUND: How did it begin?

CYNTHIA: What?

HOUND: The . . . thing.

CYNTHIA: What thing?

HOUND (*rapidly losing confidence but exasperated*): The trouble!

CYNTHIA: There hasn't *been* any trouble!

HOUND: Didn't you phone the police?

CYNTHIA: No.

FELICITY: I didn't.

MAGNUS: What for?

HOUND: I see. (*Pause.*) This puts me in a very difficult position.
(*A steady pause.*) Well, I'll be getting along, then. (*He
moves towards the door.*)

CYNTHIA: I'm terribly sorry.

HOUND (*stiffly*): That's perfectly all right.

CYNTHIA: Thank you so much for coming.

HOUND: Not at all. You never know, there might have been a
serious matter.

CYNTHIA: Drink?

HOUND: More serious than that, even.

CYNTHIA (*correcting*): Drink before you go?

HOUND: No thank you. (*Leaves.*)

CYNTHIA (*through the door*): I do hope you find him.

HOUND (*reappearing at once*): Find who, Madam?—out with it!

CYNTHIA: I thought you were looking for the lunatic.

HOUND: And what do you know about that?

CYNTHIA: It was on the radio.

HOUND: Was it, indeed? Well, that's what I'm here about, really. I didn't want to mention it because I didn't know how much you knew. No point in causing unnecessary panic, even with a murderer in our midst.

FELICITY: Murderer, did you say?

HOUND: Ah—so that was not on the radio?

CYNTHIA: Whom has he murdered, Inspector?

HOUND: Perhaps no one—yet. Let us hope we are in time.

MAGNUS: You believe he is in our midst, Inspector?

HOUND: I do. If anyone of you have recently encountered a youngish good-looking fellow in a smart suit, white shirt, hatless, well-spoken—someone possibly claiming to have just moved into the neighbourhood, someone who on the surface seems as sane as you or I, then now is the time to speak!

FELICITY: I——

HOUND: Don't interrupt!

FELICITY: Inspector——

HOUND: Very well.

CYNTHIA: No. Felicity!

HOUND: Please, Lady Cynthia, we are all in this together. I must ask you to put yourself completely in my hands.

CYNTHIA: Don't, Inspector. I love Albert.

HOUND: I don't think you quite grasp my meaning.

MAGNUS: Is one of us in danger, Inspector?

HOUND: Didn't it strike you as odd that on his escape the madman made a beeline for Muldoon Manor? It is my guess that he bears a deep-seated grudge against someone in this very house! Lady Muldoon—where is your husband?

CYNTHIA: My husband?—you don't mean——?

HOUND: I don't know—but I have a reason to believe that one of you is the real McCoy!

FELICITY: The real what?

HOUND: William Herbert McCoy who as a young man, meeting the madman in the street and being solicited for sixpence for a cup of tea, replied, "Why don't you do a decent day's work, you shifty old bag of horse manure," in Canada all those many years ago and went on to make his fortune. (*He starts to pace intensely.*) The madman was a mere boy at the time but he never forgot that moment, and thenceforth carried in his heart the promise of revenge! (*At which point he finds himself standing on top of the corpse. He looks down carefully.*)

HOUND: Is there anything you have forgotten to tell me?

(*They all see the corpse for the first time.*)

FELICITY: So the madman has struck!

CYNTHIA: Oh—it's horrible—horrible——

HOUND: Yes, just as I feared. Now you see the sort of man you are protecting.

CYNTHIA: I can't believe it!

FELICITY: I'll have to tell him, Cynthia—Inspector, a stranger of that description has indeed appeared in our midst—Simon Gascoyne. Oh, he had charm, I'll give you that, and he took me in completely. I'm afraid I made a fool of myself over him, and so did Cynthia.

HOUND: Where is he now?

MAGNUS: He must be around the house—he couldn't get away in these conditions.

HOUND: You're right. Fear naught, Lady Muldoon—I shall apprehend the man who killed your husband.

CYNTHIA: My husband? I don't understand.

HOUND: Everything points to Gascoyne.

CYNTHIA: But who's that? (*The corpse.*)

HOUND: Your husband.

CYNTHIA: No, it's not.

HOUND: Yes, it is.

CYNTHIA: I tell you it's not.

HOUND: *I'm* in charge of this case!

CYNTHIA: But that's not my husband.

HOUND: Are you sure?

CYNTHIA: For goodness sake!

HOUND: Then who is it?

CYNTHIA: I don't know.

HOUND: Anybody?

FELICITY: I've never seen him before.

MAGNUS: Quite unlike anybody I've ever met.

HOUND: This case is becoming an utter shambles.

CYNTHIA: But what are we going to do?

HOUND (*snatching the phone*): I'll phone the police!

CYNTHIA: But you are the police!

HOUND: Thank God I'm here—the lines have been cut!

CYNTHIA: You mean——?

HOUND: Yes!—we're on our own, cut off from the world and in grave danger!

FELICITY: You mean——?

HOUND: Yes!—I think the killer will strike again!

MAGNUS: You mean——?

HOUND: Yes! One of us ordinary mortals thrown together by fate and cut off by the elements, is the murderer! He must be found—search the house!

> (*All depart speedily in different directions leaving a momentarily empty stage. SIMON strolls on.*)

SIMON (*entering, calling*): Anyone about?—funny. . . .

> (*He notices the corpse and is surprised. He approaches it and turns it over. He stands up and looks about in alarm.*)

BIRDBOOT: This is where Simon gets the chop.

> (*There is a shot. SIMON falls dead.*)
>
> (*INSPECTOR HOUND runs on and crouches down by SIMON's body. CYNTHIA appears at the french windows. She stops there and stares.*)

CYNTHIA: What happened, Inspector?!

> (*HOUND turns to face her.*)

HOUND: He's dead. . . . Simon Gascoyne, I presume. Rough justice even for a killer—unless—unless—We assumed that the body could not have been lying there before Simon Gascoyne entered the house . . . but . . . (*he slides the sofa over the body*) there's your answer. And now—who killed

bunny-boo—— Now for God's sake—— Good-bye, Myrtle
—(*puts down phone*).

(BIRDBOOT *mops his brow with his handkerchief. As he turns,
a tennis ball bounces into through the french windows,
followed by* FELICITY, *as before, in tennis outfit. The lighting
is as it was. Everything is as it was. It is, let us say, the same
moment of time.*)

FELICITY (*calling*): Out! (*She catches sight of* BIRDBOOT *and is
amazed.*) You!

BIRDBOOT: Er, yes—hello again.

FELICITY: What are you doing here?!

BIRDBOOT: Well, I . . .

FELICITY: Honestly, darling, you really are extraordinary——

BIRDBOOT: Yes, well, here I am. (*He looks round sheepishly.*)

FELICITY: You must have been desperate to see me—I mean, I'm
flattered, but couldn't it wait till I got back?

BIRDBOOT: No, no, you've got it all wrong——

FELICITY: What is it?

BIRDBOOT: And about last night—perhaps I gave you the wrong
impression—got carried away a bit, perhaps——

FELICITY (*stiffly*): What are you trying to say?

BIRDBOOT: I want to call it off.

FELICITY: I see.

BIRDBOOT: I didn't promise anything—and the fact is, I have my
reputation—people do talk——

FELICITY: You don't have to say any more——

BIRDBOOT: And my wife, too—I don't know how she got to hear
of it, but——

FELICITY: Of all the nerve! To march in here and——

BIRDBOOT: I'm sorry you had to find out like this—the fact is I
didn't mean it this way——

FELICITY: You philandering coward!

BIRDBOOT: I'm sorry—but I want you to know that I meant those
things I said—oh yes—shows brilliant promise—I shall
say so——

FELICITY: I'll kill you for this, Simon Gascoyne!

(*She leaves in tears, passing* MRS. DRUDGE *who has entered in time to overhear her last remark.*)

BIRDBOOT (*wide-eyed*): Good God. . . .

MRS. DRUDGE: I have come to set up the card table, sir.

BIRDBOOT (*wildly*): I can't stay for a game of *cards*!

MRS. DRUDGE: Oh, Lady Muldoon *will* be disappointed.

BIRDBOOT: You mean . . . you mean, she wants to meet me. . . ?

MRS. DRUDGE: Oh yes, sir, I just told her and it put her in quite a tizzy.

BIRDBOOT: Really? Yes, well, a man of my influence is not to be sneezed at—I think I have some small name for the making of reputations—mmm, yes, quite a tizzy, you say?

(MRS. DRUDGE *is busied with the card table.* BIRDBOOT *stands marooned and bemused for a moment.*)

MOON (*from his seat*): Birdboot!—(*a tense whisper*). Birdboot!
(BIRDBOOT *looks round vaguely.*)
What the hell are you doing?

BIRDBOOT: Nothing.

MOON: Stop making an ass of yourself. Come back.

BIRDBOOT: Oh, I know what you're thinking—but the fact is I genuinely consider her performance to be one of the summits——

(CYNTHIA *enters as before.* MRS. DRUDGE *has gone.*)

CYNTHIA: Darling!

BIRDBOOT: Ah, good evening—may I say that I genuinely consider——

CYNTHIA: Don't say anything for a moment—just hold me.
(*She falls into his arms.*)

BIRDBOOT: All right! (*They kiss.*) My God!—she *does* have her mouth open! Dear lady, from the first moment I saw you, I felt my whole life changing——

CYNTHIA (*breaking free*): We can't go on meeting like this!

BIRDBOOT: I am not ashamed to proclaim nightly my love for you!—but fortunately that will not be necessary—— I know of a very good hotel, discreet—run by a man of the world——

CYNTHIA: But darling, this is madness!

BIRDBOOT: Yes! I am mad with love.

CYNTHIA: Please!—remember where we are!

BIRDBOOT: I don't care! Let them think what they like, I love you!

CYNTHIA: Don't—I love Albert!

BIRDBOOT: He's dead. (*Shaking her.*) Do you understand me—Albert's dead!

CYNTHIA: No—I'll never give up hope! Let me go! We are not free!

BIRDBOOT: You mean Myrtle? She means nothing to me—nothing!—she's all cocoa and blue nylon fur slippers—not a spark of creative genius in her whole slumping knee-length-knickered body——

CYNTHIA: You're a cad, Simon! You will use me and cast me aside as you have cast aside so many others!

BIRDBOOT: No, Cynthia—now that I have found you——

CYNTHIA: You're ruthless—so strong—so cruel——

(BIRDBOOT *seizes her in an embrace, during which* MRS. DRUDGE *enters, and* MOON'S *fevered voice is heard.*)

MOON: Have you taken leave of your tiny mind?

(CYNTHIA *breaks free.*)

CYNTHIA: Stop—can't you see you're making a fool of yourself!

MOON: She's right.

BIRDBOOT (*to* MOON): You keep out of this.

CYNTHIA: Yes, what is it, Mrs. Drudge?

MRS. DRUDGE: Should I close the windows, my lady? The fog——

CYNTHIA: Yes, you'd better.

MOON: Look, they've got your number——

BIRDBOOT: I'll leave in my own time, thank you very much.

MOON: It's the finish of you, I suppose you know that——

BIRDBOOT: I don't need your twopenny Grubb Street prognostications—I have found something bigger and finer——

MOON: (*bemused, to himself*): If only it were Higgs. . . .

CYNTHIA: . . . And fetch the Major down.

MRS. DRUDGE: I think I hear him coming down stairs now.

(*She leaves. The sound of a wheelchair's approach as before.* BIRDBOOT *prudently keeps out of the chair's former path but it enters from the next wing down and knocks him flying. A babble of anguish and protestation.*)

CYNTHIA: Simon—say something!

BIRDBOOT: That reckless bastard (*as he sits up*).

CYNTHIA: Thank God!——

MAGNUS: What's *he* doing here?

CYNTHIA: He just turned up.

MAGNUS: Really? How do you like it here?

BIRDBOOT: I couldn't take it night after night.

(FELICITY *enters.*)

FELICITY: So—you're still here.

CYNTHIA: Of course he's still here. We're going to play cards.
There is no need to introduce you two, is there, for I recall
now that you, Simon, met me through Felicity, our mutual
friend.

FELICITY: Yes, Simon is an old friend——

BIRDBOOT: Ah—yes—well, I like to give young up and comers the
benefit of my—er—Of course, she lacks technique as yet——

FELICITY: Last night.

BIRDBOOT: I'm not talking about last night!

CYNTHIA: Indeed? Well, you deal, Felicity. Simon, you help me
with the sofa.

BIRDBOOT (*to* MOON): Did you see that? Tried to kill me. I told
you it was Magnus—not that it *is* Magnus.

MOON: Who did it, you mean?

BIRDBOOT: What?

MOON: You think it's not Magnus who did it?

BIRDBOOT: Get a grip on yourself, Moon—the facts are staring
you in the face. He's after Cynthia for one thing.

MAGNUS: It's Gascoyne, isn't it?

BIRDBOOT: Over my dead body!

MAGNUS: If he comes between us . . .

MOON (*angrily*): For God's sake sit down!

CYNTHIA: Simon!

BIRDBOOT: She needs me, Moon. I've got to make up a four.

(CYNTHIA *and* BIRDBOOT *move the sofa as before, and they all
sit at the table.*)

CYNTHIA: Right! Who starts?

MAGNUS: I do. I'll dummy for a no-bid ruff and double my holding on South's queen. (*While he moves cards.*)

CYNTHIA. Did I hear you say you saw Felicity last night, Simon?

BIRDBOOT: Er—er——

FELICITY: Pay twenty-ones or trump my contract. (*Discards.*) Cynthia's turn.

CYNTHIA: I'll trump your contract with five dummy no-trumps there (*discards*), and I'll move West's rook for the re-bid with a banker ruff on his second trick there. (*Discards.*) Simon?

BIRDBOOT: Would you mind doing that again?

CYNTHIA: And I'll ruff your dummy with five no-bid trumps there, (*discards*) and I support your re-bid with a banker for the solo ruff in the dummy trick there. (*discards.*)

BIRDBOOT (*standing up and throwing down his cards*): And I call your bluff!

CYNTHIA: Well done, Simon!

(MAGNUS *pays* BIRDBOOT *while* CYNTHIA *deals.*)

FELICITY: Strange how Simon appeared in the neighbourhood from nowhere, we know so little about him.

CYNTHIA: Right, Simon, it's your opening on the minor bid. Hmm. Let's see. I think I'll overbid the spade convention with two no-trumps and King's gambit offered there— (*discards*) and West's dummy split double to Queen's Bishop four there!

MAGNUS (*as he plays cards*): Faites vos jeux. Rien ne va plus. Rouge et noir. Zero.

CYNTHIA: Simon?

BIRDBOOT (*triumphant, leaping to his feet*) And I call your bluff!

CYNTHIA (*imperturbably*): I meld.

FELICITY: I huff.

MAGNUS: I ruff.

BIRDBOOT: I bluff.

CYNTHIA: Twist.

FELICITY: Bust.

MAGNUS. Check.

BIRDBOOT: Snap.

CYNTHIA: How's that?

FELICITY: Not out.

MAGNUS: Double top.

BIRDBOOT: Bingo!

CYNTHIA: No! Simon—your luck's in tonight.

FELICITY: We shall see—the night is not over yet, Simon Gascoyne! (*She quickly exits.*)

BIRDBOOT (*looking after* FELICITY): Red herring—smell it a mile off. (*To* MAGNUS.) Oh, yes, she's as clean as a whistle, I've seen it a thousand times. And I've seen you before too, haven't I? Strange—there's something about you——

MAGNUS: Care for a spin round the rose garden, Cynthia?

CYNTHIA: No, Magnus, I must talk to Simon.

BIRDBOOT: There's nothing for you there, you know.

MAGNUS: You think so?

BIRDBOOT: Oh, yes, she knows which side her bread is buttered. I am a man not without a certain influence among those who would reap the limelight—she's not going to throw me over for a heavily disguised cripple.

MAGNUS. There's an old Canadian proverb——

BIRDBOOT: Don't give me that—I tumbled to you right from the start—oh, yes, you chaps are not as clever as you think. . . . Sooner or later you make your mistake. . . . Incidentally, where was it I saw you? . . . I've definitely——

MAGNUS (*leaving*): Well, I think I'll go and oil my gun. (*Exit.*)

BIRDBOOT (*after* MAGNUS): Double bluff!—(*to* CYNTHIA) I've seen it a thousand times.

CYNTHIA: I think Magnus suspects something. And Felicity? Simon, was there anything between you and Felicity?

BIRDBOOT: No, no—that's all over now. I merely flattered her a a little over a drink, told her she'd go far, that sort of thing. Dear me, the fuss that's been made over a simple flirtation——

CYNTHIA (*as* MRS. DRUDGE *enters behind*): If I find you have falsely seduced me from my dear husband Albert, I will kill you, Simon Gascoyne!

(*The* "CURTAIN" *as before.* MRS. DRUDGE *and* CYNTHIA

leave. BIRDBOOT *starts to follow them.*)

MOON: *Birdboot!*

(BIRDBOOT *stops.*)

MOON: For God's sake pull yourself together.

BIRDBOOT: I can't help it.

MOON: What do you think you're doing? You're turning it into a complete farce!

BIRDBOOT: I know, I know—but I can't live without her. (*He is making erratic neurotic journeys about the stage.*) I shall resign my position, of course. I don't care I'm a gonner, I tell you—— (*He has arrived at the body. He looks at it in surprise, hesitates, bends and turns it over.*)

MOON: Birdboot, think of your family, your friends—your high standing the world of letters—I say, what are you doing? (BIRDBOOT *is staring at the body's face.*)

Birdboot . . . leave it alone. Come and sit down—what's the matter with you?

BIRDBOOT (*dead-voiced*): It's Higgs.

MOON: What?

BIRDBOOT: It's Higgs.

(*Pause.*)

MOON: Don't be silly.

BIRDBOOT: I tell you it's Higgs!

(MOON *half rises. Bewildered.*)

I don't understand. . . . He's dead.

MOON: Dead?

BIRDBOOT: Who would want to. . . ?

MOON: He must have been lying there all the time. . . .

BIRDBOOT: . . . kill Higgs?

MOON: But what's he doing here? I was standing in tonight. . . .

BIRDBOOT (*turning*): Moon? . . .

MOON (*in wonder, quietly*): So it's me and Puckeridge now.

BIRDBOOT: *Moon . . . ?*

MOON (*faltering*): But I swear I. . . .

BIRDBOOT: I've got it——

MOON: But I didn't——

BIRDBOOT (*quietly*): My God . . . so that was it. . . . (*Up.*) Moon
    —now I see——

MOON: —I swear I didn't——

BIRDBOOT: Now—finally—I see it all——
    (*There is a shot and* BIRDBOOT *falls dead.*)

MOON: Birdboot! (*He runs on, to* BIRDBOOT'*s body.*)
    (CYNTHIA *appears at the french windows. She stops and
    stares. All as before.*)

CYNTHIA: Oh my God—what happened, Inspector?

MOON (*almost to himself*): He's dead. . . . (*He rises.*) That's a bit
    rough, isn't it?—A bit extreme!—He may have had his faults
    —I admit he was a fickle old . . . Who did this, and why?
    (MOON *turns to face her. He stands up and makes swiftly for
    his seat. Before he gets there he is stopped by the sound of
    voices.*)
    (SIMON *and* HOUND *are occupying the critics' seats.*)
    (MOON *freezes.*)

SIMON: To say that it is without pace, point, focus, interest,
    drama, wit or originality is to say simply that it does not
    happen to be my cup of tea. One has only to compare this
    ragbag with the masters of the genre to see that here we
    have a trifle that is not my cup of tea at all.

HOUND: I'm sorry to be blunt but there is no getting away from
    it. It lacks pace. A complete ragbag.

SIMON: I will go further. Those of you who were fortunate
    enough to be at the Comedie Française on Wednesday last,
    will not need to be reminded that hysterics are no substitute
    for *éclat*

HOUND: It lacks *élan*.

SIMON: Some of the cast seem to have given up acting altogether,
    apparently aghast, with every reason, at finding themselves
    involved in an evening that would, and indeed will, make
    the angels weep.

HOUND: I am not a prude but I fail to see any reason for the
    shower of filth and sexual allusion foisted on to an un-
    suspecting public in the guise of modernity at all costs. . . .
    (*Behind* MOON, FELICITY, MAGNUS *and* MRS. DRUDGE *have*

made their entrances, so that he turns to face their semi-circle.)

MAGNUS (*pointing to* BIRDBOOT's *body*): Well, Inspector, is this your man?

MOON (*warily*): . . . Yes. . . . Yes. . . .

CYNTHIA: It's Simon . . .

MOON: Yes . . . yes . . . poor. . . . (*Up.*) Is this some kind of a joke?

MAGNUS: If it is, Inspector, it's in very poor taste.

(MOON *pulls himself together and becomes galvanic, a little wild, in grief for* BIRDBOOT.)

MOON: All right! I'm going to find out who did this! I want everyone to go to the positions they occupied when the shot was fired—(*they move; hysterically*): No one will leave the house! (*They move back.*)

MAGNUS: I think we all had the opportunity to fire the shot, Inspector——

MOON (*furious*): I am not——

MAGNUS: —but which of us would want to?

MOON: Perhaps you, Major Magnus!

MAGNUS: Why should I want to kill him?

MOON: Because he was on to you—yes, he tumbled you right from the start—and you shot him just when he was about to reveal that you killed—(MOON *points, pauses and then crosses to* Higgs's *body and falters*)—killed—(*he turns* Higgs *over*)—this . . . chap.

MAGNUS: But what motive would there be for killing him? (*Pause.*) Who *is* this chap? (*Pause.*) Inspector?

MOON (*rising*): I don't know. Quite unlike anyone I've ever met. (*Long pause.*) Well . . . now . . .

MRS. DRUDGE: Inspector?

MOON (*eagerly*): Yes? Yes, what is it, dear lady?

MRS. DRUDGE: Happening to enter this room earlier in the day to close the windows, I chanced to overhear a remark made by the deceased Simon Gascoyne to her ladyship, viz.—"I will kill anyone who comes between us."

MOON: Ah—yes—well, that's it, then. This . . . chap . . .

(*pointing*) was obviously killed by (*pointing*) er . . .
by (*pause*) Simon.

CYNTHIA: But he didn't come between us!

MAGNUS: And who, then, killed Simon?

MRS. DRUDGE: Subsequent to that reported remark, I also
happened to be in earshot of a remark made by Lady
Muldoon to the deceased, to the effect, "I will kill you,
Simon Gascoyne!" I hope you don't mind my mentioning it.

MOON: Not at all. I'm glad you did. It is from these chance
remarks that we in the force build up our complete picture
before moving in to make the arrest. It will not be long now,
I fancy, and I must warn you, Lady Muldoon that anything
you say——

CYNTHIA: Yes!—I hated Simon Gascoyne, for he had me in his
power!—But I didn't kill him!

MRS. DRUDGE: Prior to that, Inspector, I also chanced to overhear a remark made by Miss Cunningham, no doubt in
the heat of the moment, but it stuck in my mind as these
things do, viz., "I will kill you for this, Simon Gascoyne!"

MOON: Ah! The final piece of the jigsaw! I think I am now in a
position to reveal the mystery. This man (*the corpse*) was,
of course, McCoy, the Canadian who, as we heard, meeting
Gascoyne in the street and being solicited for sixpence for a
toffee apple, smacked him across the ear, with the cry,
"How's that for a grudge to harbour, you sniffling little
workshy!" all those many years ago. Gascoyne bided his
time, but in due course tracked McCoy down to this
house, having, on the way, met, in the neighbourhood, a
simple ambitious girl from the provinces. He was charming,
persuasive—told her, I have no doubt, that she would go
straight to the top—and she, flattered by his sophistication,
taken in by his promises to see her all right on the night,
gave in to his simple desires. Perhaps she loved him. We
shall never know. But in the very hour of her promised
triumph, his eye fell on another—yes, I refer to Lady
Cynthia Muldoon. From the moment he caught sight of her
there was no other woman for him—he was in her spell,

willing to sacrifice anything, even you, Felicity Cunningham.
It was only today—unexpectedly finding him here—that
you learned the truth. There was a bitter argument which
ended with your promise to kill him—a promise that you
carried out in this very room at your first opportunity! And
I must warn you that anything you say——

FELICITY: But it doesn't make sense!

MOON: Not at first glance, *perhaps*.

MAGNUS: Could not Simon have been killed by the same person
who killed McCoy?

FELICITY: But why should any of us want to kill a perfect stranger?

MAGNUS: Perhaps he was not a stranger to *one* of us.

MOON (*faltering*): But Simon was the madman, wasn't he?

MAGNUS: We only have your word for that, Inspector. We only
have your word for a lot of things. For instance—McCoy.
Who is he? Is his name McCoy? Is there any truth in that
fantastic and implausible tale of the insult inflicted in the
Canadian streets? Or is there something else, something
quite unknown to us, behind all this? Suppose for a moment
that the madman, having killed this unknown stranger for
private and inscrutable reasons of his own, was disturbed
before he could dispose of the body, so having cut the
telephone wires he decided to return to the scene of the
crime, masquerading as—Police Inspector Hound!

MOON: But . . . I'm not mad . . . I'm almost sure I'm not mad. . . .

MAGNUS: . . . only to discover that in the house was a man,
Simon Gascoyne, who recognized the corpse as a man against
whom you had held a deep-seated grudge——!

MOON: But I didn't kill—I'm almost sure I——

MAGNUS: I put it to you!—are you the real Inspector Hound?!

MOON: You know damn well I'm not! What's it all about?

MAGNUS: I thought as much.

MOON: I only dreamed . . . sometimes I dreamed——

CYNTHIA: So it was you!

MRS. DRUDGE: The madman!

FELICITY: The killer!

CYNTHIA: Oh, it's horrible, horrible.

MRS. DRUDGE: The stranger in our midst!

MAGNUS: Yes, we had a shrewd suspicion he would turn up here
—and he walked into the trap!

MOON: What *trap*?

MAGNUS: I am not the real Magnus Muldoon!—It was a mere
subterfuge!—and (*standing up and removing his moustaches*)
I now reveal myself as——

CYNTHIA: You mean——?

MAGNUS: Yes!—I am the real Inspector Hound!

MOON (*pause*): *Puckeridge!*

MAGNUS (*with pistol*): Stand where you are, or I shoot!

MOON (*backing*): Puckeridge! You killed Higgs—and Birdboot
tried to tell me——

MAGNUS: Stop in the name of the law!

(MOON *turns to run.* MAGNUS *fires.* MOON *drops to his knees.*)
I have waited a long time for this moment.

CYNTHIA: So you are the real Inspector Hound.

MAGNUS: Not only that!—I have been leading a double life—at
least!

CYNTHIA: You mean——?

MAGNUS: Yes!—It's been ten long years, but don't you know me?

CYNTHIA: You mean——?

MAGNUS: Yes!—it is me, Albert!—who lost his memory and
joined the force, rising by merit to the rank of Inspector,
his past blotted out—until fate cast him back into the home
he left behind, back to the beautiful woman he had brought
here as his girlish bride—in short, my darling, my memory
has returned and your long wait is over!

CYNTHIA: Oh, Albert!

(*They embrace.*)

MOON (*with a trace of admiration*): Puckeridge . . . you cunning
bastard.

(MOON *dies.*)

THE END

AFTER MAGRITTE

CHARACTERS

HARRIS	aged about 40
THELMA	his wife, a bit younger, attractive
MOTHER	a little old, tough, querulous lady
FOOT	Detective Inspector
HOLMES	Police Constable

The first performance of *After Magritte* was given at the Ambiance Lunch-hour Theatre Club on 9 April 1970. The cast was as follows:

FOOT	Clive Barker
HOLMES	Malcolm Ingram
HARRIS	Stephen Moore
THELMA	Prunella Scales
MOTHER	Josephine Tewson

Directed by Geoffrey Reeves

SCENE

A room. Early evening.

    The only light is that which comes through the large window which is facing the audience. The street door is in the same upstage wall. There is another door on each side of the stage, leading to the rest of the flat.

    The central ceiling light hangs from a long flex which disappears up into the flies. The lampshade itself is a heavy metal hemisphere, opaque, poised about eight feet from the floor.

    A yard or more to one side (Stage L), and similarly hanging from the flies, is a fruit basket attractively overflowing with apples, oranges, bananas, pineapple, and grapes. The cord or flex is tied round the handle of the basket.

    It will become apparent that the light fixture is on a counterweight system; it can be raised or lowered, or kept in any vertical position, by means of the counterbalance, which in this case is a basket of fruit.

    Most of the furniture is stacked up against the street door in a sort of barricade. An essential item is a long low bench-type table, about eight feet long, but the pile also includes a settee, two comfortable chairs, a TV set, a cupboard and a wind-up gramophone with an old-fashioned horn. The cupboard is probably the item on which stand the telephone and a deep-shaded table lamp, unlit but connected to a wall plug.

    Directly under the central light is a wooden chair. Hanging over the back of the chair is a black tail-coat, a white dress shirt and a white bow-tie. Towards Stage R, in profile, is an ironing board with its iron upended on the asbestos mat at the centre-stage end of the board.

    There is no other furniture.

    There are three people in the room.

    MOTHER *is lying on her back on the ironing board, her head to Stage R, her downstage foot up against the flat of the iron. A white bath towel covers her from ankle to chin. Her head and part of her face are concealed in a tight-fitting black rubber bathing cap. A black bowler hat reposes on her stomach. She could be dead; but is not.*

    THELMA HARRIS *is dressed in a full-length ballgown and her hair is expensively 'up'. She looks as though she is ready to go out to a dance, which she is. Her silver shoes, however, are not on her feet: they have been discarded somewhere on the floor.* THELMA *is discovered on her hands and knees, in profile to the audience, staring at the floor ahead and giving vent to an occasional sniff.*

REGINALD HARRIS *is standing on the wooden chair. His torso is bare, but underneath his thigh-length green rubber fishing waders he wears his black evening dress trousers. His hands are at his sides. His head is tilted back directly below the lampshade, which hangs a foot or two above him, and he is blowing slowly and deliberately up into the recess of the shade.*

Gazing at this scene through the window is a uniformed Police Constable (HOLMES). *Only his shoulders, his face and his helmet are visible above the sill. He stands absolutely motionless, and might be a cut-out figure; but is not.*

For several seconds there is no movement, and no sound save the occasional sniffing from THELMA. THELMA *pads forward a couple of paces, still scanning the floor ahead and around.* HARRIS *blows into the lampshade.*

Without looking up at HARRIS, THELMA *speaks.*

THELMA: It's electric, dear.

HARRIS: (*mildly*) I didn't think it was a flaming torch.

THELMA: There's no need to use language. That's what I always say.

> (*She pads on a bit, scanning the floor.* HARRIS *tries to remove the light bulb but it is apparently still too hot: he blows on his sharply withdrawn fingers, and then continues to blow on the light bulb. After a couple of blows he tests the bulb again and is able to remove it.*
> *This upsets the delicate balance of the counterweight. The shade, relieved of the weight of the bulb, slowly begins to ascend, while the basket of fruit descends accordingly.* HARRIS, *however, has anticipated this and the movement is one of only a few inches before he has turned on his chair and removed an apple from the basket. This reverses the effect: the basket ascends, the shade descends. But* HARRIS *has anticipated this also: he takes a bite out of the apple and replaces it. The equilibrium is thus restored.*)
> You could have used your handkerchief.

HARRIS: (*intrigued*) You mean, *semaphore*?

(*But* THELMA *is not listening: she has given up her search, stood up, approached her shoes—and stepped on something; it is in fact a lead slug from a .22 calibre pistol. She picks it up with satisfaction and tosses it into a metal wastebin wherein it makes the appropriate sound.*)

THELMA: A hundred and forty-nine.

(*She hands the iron's plug up to* HARRIS *and accepts from him the warm bulb.*)

HARRIS: I never took semaphore as a sophomore, morse the pity.

(THELMA *looks at him icily but he has his own cool.*)

I used the time in a vain attempt to get the Rockefeller girl to marry me for my sense of humour. Would you pass my hat?

(THELMA *passes him the bowler hat, which he puts on his head. He then inserts the iron plug into the light socket, deftly removing his hat and hanging it on a banana, thus cancelling out the imbalance threatened by the weight of the plug and its flex.* THELMA's *attention does not stay to be impressed.*)

THELMA: For some reason, my mind keeps returning to that one-legged footballer we passed in the car . . . What *position* do you suppose he plays?

(HARRIS *has got down off the chair and looked critically around.*)

HARRIS: Bit dark in here.

(*The natural light from the window is indeed somewhat inadequate.* THELMA *pursues her own thoughts and a path to the light switch, positioned by the door at Stage L, which controls the ceiling light, or, at the moment, the iron.*)

THELMA: I keep thinking about him. What guts he must have!

HARRIS: Put the light on.

(THELMA *independently depresses the light switch, and the red warm-up light on the iron comes on.* HARRIS *regards it sceptically.*)

Most unsatisfactory.

THELMA: I mean, what fantastic *pluck*! What real never-say-die *spirit*, you know what I mean? (*Pause.*) Bloody unfair on the rest of the team, mind you—you'd think the decent thing would have been to hang up his boot. *What are you doing now?!*

(*For* HARRIS *has gone upstage to the table lamp resting amid the
barricade and tried, without result, to turn it on, whereupon he
has started to blow violently against the shade. He replies
immediately.*)

HARRIS: Filthy. Hasn't been dusted for weeks. I could write my
name on it. (*He proceeds to do so, in full, remarking the while:*)
It wasn't a football, it was a turtle.

THELMA: A turtle?

HARRIS: Or a large tortoise.

THELMA: *What?*

HARRIS: He was carrying a tortoise.

THELMA: You must be blind.

HARRIS: (*equably*) It was he who was blind. What happened to the
bulb?
(*He means the bulb from the table lamp.*
THELMA *however, holds out the warm bulb.*)

THELMA: Here.

HARRIS: What did you take the bulb out for?

THELMA: No, that was the one you put in the bathroom. *This* is
the one which——
(*As he takes the bulb from her by the metal end and flips it angrily
into the air, catching it by the glass.*)
——you just took out——

HARRIS: (*shouts*) Not by the metal end! (*Irritably he goes to insert
the bulb into the table lamp.*)

THELMA: And how do you explain the West Bromwich Albion
football shirt?

HARRIS: Pyjamas—he was wearing pyjamas. (*He successfully
switches on the lamp, raising the gloom considerably as he gazes
moodily around. He continues to speak, characteristically,
without punctuation.*) This place is run like a madhouse.
What's that policeman staring at?
(THELMA *turns to the window, marches up to it and viciously
draws the curtains together.*)

THELMA: Bloody nerve!
(*There is a piercing scream, from* MOTHER *as she jerks her foot
away from the heated-up iron. This causes some confusion and
cries of pain from* MOTHER *and cries of 'Mother!' from*

THELMA, *who snatches up the iron and places it on the wooden chair, the fruit adjusting itself accordingly.* MOTHER *is now sitting up on the irioning board, facing the audience, her burned foot clutched in her lap, the other hanging down. Her first audible word seems to be a vulgarity; but is not.*)

MOTHER: *Butter!*

THELMA: (*primly*) Now there's no need to use language——

MOTHER: Get some butter!

THELMA: *Butter!*—Get butter, Reginald!

(HARRIS *rushes out.* THELMA *grabs the phone.*)

(*Dialling*) Don't move—whatever you do don't move—Hello!—I want an ambulance! (*There is a loud knocking on the door.* THELMA *drops the phone—it falls into the cradle—and rushes to the window, shouting.*) Who is it?

(*She draws back the curtains, and the Policeman reappears.*)

HOLMES: It's the police!

THELMA: (*furiously*) I asked for an ambulance!

(*She viciously draws the curtains together and dashes back to pick up the phone.*

HARRIS *rushes in with half a pound of soft butter on a butter dish.*)

HARRIS: Where do you want it, mother?

MOTHER: On my foot, you nincompoop.

(HARRIS *slams the butter up against the sole of* MOTHER's *undamaged foot.*

The confusion ceases at once. THELMA *replaces the phone and stands quietly.* HARRIS *stands up looking slightly crestfallen.* MOTHER *regards him glacially. There is a silence.*) You married a fool, Thelma.

(MOTHER *gets down on the floor, on her good, though buttered, foot.*) Has the bathroom light been repaired?

HARRIS: I put in a new bulb, mother.

MOTHER: I hope you cleaned your boots. (MOTHER *hops one-legged across the stage to the door and leaves, not before delivering the following threat.*) I shall be back for my practice. (*Certain things are integrated with the following dialogue. The iron goes back on the ironing board. The fruit adjusts.* THELMA *irons the white dress shirt while* HARRIS, *sitting on the wooden*

> *chair, takes off his waders, which have been concealing not only*
> *his trousers but his black patent leather shoes.* HARRIS *crams the*
> *waders into the cupboard in the barricade of furniture.*
> *When the shirt has been ironed,* HARRIS *puts it on, and puts on*
> *the bow-tie, and finally the coat. After ironing,* HARRIS *climbs*
> *back on the wooden chair to remove the iron plug and, of course,*
> *the bowler hat, which, for want of anywhere else, he puts on his*
> *head.* MOTHER *leaves the room.*)

HARRIS: Don't start blaming me. She could have lain on the floor.

THELMA: Oh yes—very nice—with my back in the state it's
in—you'd rather I bent double.

HARRIS: You could have squatted over her. It's not *my* fault that
the furniture could not be put to its proper use in its proper
place.

THELMA: *If* you're referring to the Cricklewood Lyceum——

HARRIS: I *am* referring to the Cricklewood Lyceum—it was a
fiasco——

THELMA: You know perfectly well that my foot got caught in my
hem——

HARRIS: With *your* legs?—your feet don't *reach* your hem.

THELMA: My legs are insured for £5,000!

HARRIS: Only against theft. The fact of the matter is, it was a
botch from first to last, and that is why we find ourselves
having to go through it again at the eleventh hour, half of
which has now gone. *We are never going to get away on time!*

THELMA: (*ironing the shirt*) I am being as quick as I can. All I can
say is I'll be glad when it's all over and things are back to
normal. It's making you short-tempered and argumentative.
You contradict everything I say——

HARRIS: (*heatedly*) *That* I deny——

THELMA: I've only got to mention that the footballer had a
football under his arm and you start insisting it was a
tortoise. Why a footballer should play with a tortoise is a
question which you don't seem prepared to face.

HARRIS: (*calmingly, reasonably*) Look—he was not a footballer.
He was just a chap in striped pyjamas. It was a perfectly
natural, not to say uninteresting, mistake and it led you to
the further and even more boring misapprehension that what

he was carrying was a football—whereas *I*——

THELMA: Whereas you, accepting as a matter of course a pyjama-clad figure in the street, leap to the natural conclusion that he must be carrying a tortoise.

HARRIS: The man obviously had his reasons.

THELMA: You've got to admit that a football is more likely.

HARRIS: More likely?

THELMA: In the sense that there would be more footballs than tortoises in a built-up area.

HARRIS: Leaving aside the fact that your premise is far from self-evident, it is more *likely*, by that criterion, that what the fellow had under his arm was a Christmas pudding or a copy of Whitaker's Almanac, but I happened to see him with my own eyes——

THELMA: We all saw him——

HARRIS: —and he was an old man with one leg and a white beard, dressed in pyjamas, hopping along in the rain with a tortoise under his arm and brandishing a white stick to clear a path through those gifted with sight——

THELMA: There was no one else on the pavement.

HARRIS: Since he was blind he could hardly be expected to know that.

THELMA: Who said he was blind? *You* say so——

HARRIS: (heatedly) He had a white stick, woman!

THELMA: (equably) In my opinion it was an ivory cane.

HARRIS: (shouting) An ivory cane IS a white stick!! (*This seems to exhaust them both.* THELMA *irons placidly, though still rebellious. After a while . . .*)

THELMA: (scornfully) Pyjamas . . . I suppose he was hopping in his sleep. Yes, I can see it now—a bad dream—he leaps to his foot, grabs his tortoise and feels his way into the street——

HARRIS: I am only telling you what I saw! And I suggest to you that a blind one-legged white-bearded footballer would have a hard time keeping his place in West Bromwich Albion.

THELMA: He was a young chap.

HARRIS: (patiently) He had a white beard.

THELMA: Shaving foam.

HARRIS: (leaping up) Have you taken leave of your senses?

THELMA: (*strongly*) It was shaving foam! In pyjamas, if you insist,
striped in the colours of West Bromwich Albion, if you
allow, carrying under his arm, if not a football then
something very similar like a wineskin or a pair of bagpipes,
and swinging a white stick in the form of an ivory cane——

HARRIS: Bagpipes?

THELMA: —*but what he had on his face was definitely shaving foam!*
(*Pause.*) Or possibly some kind of yashmak.
(HARRIS *is almost speechless.*)

HARRIS: The most—*the very most*—I am prepared to concede is
that he *may* have been a sort of street arab making off with
his lute—*but young he was not and white-bearded he was!*

THELMA: His *loot*?

HARRIS: (*expansively*) Or his mandolin—Who's to say?

THELMA: You admit he could have been musical?

HARRIS: I admit nothing of the sort! As a matter of fact, if he had
been an Arab musician, the likelihood is that he would have
been carrying a gourd—which is very much the shape and
size of a tortoise, which strongly suggests that I was right in
my initial conjecture: white beard, white stick, pyjamas,
tortoise. I refuse to discuss it any further.

THELMA: You'll never admit you're wrong, will you?

HARRIS: On the contrary, if I were ever wrong I would be the *first*
to admit it. But these outlandish embellishments of yours are
gratuitous and strain the credulity.

THELMA: (*sighing*) We should have stopped and taken a
photograph. Then we wouldn't be having these arguments.

HARRIS: (*morosely*) We wouldn't be having them if we'd stayed at
home, as I myself wished to do.

THELMA: It was for mother's benefit, not yours. She doesn't often
ask to be taken anywhere, and it didn't cost you much to let
her have her pleasure.

HARRIS: It cost me ten shillings in parking tickets alone.

THELMA: It was only one ticket, and it was your own fault for not
putting any money in the meter. The truth is that we are very
fortunate that a woman of her age still has an active interest,
even if it is the tuba.

HARRIS: Active interest?—she's an obsessed woman; dragging us

half way across London—you'd think having one in the
house and playing it morning, noon and night would be
enough for anyone. It's certainly too much for me.

THELMA: She's entitled to practise, just as much as we are.

HARRIS: But it's our house.

THELMA: You shouldn't have asked her to move in if you felt like
that.

HARRIS: It was your idea.

THELMA: You agreed to it.

HARRIS: I agreed to her living out her last days among her loved
ones—I said nothing about having her underfoot for half a
lifetime.

THELMA: You said it would be useful for baby-sitting.

HARRIS: We haven't got any *children*!

THELMA: That's hardly her fault. (*Pause.*) Or mine.
(HARRIS *gets slowly to his feet.*)

HARRIS: How dare you? How *dare* you! Right—that's it! I've put
up with a lot of slanders but my indulgence is now at an end.
This is my house and you can tell your mother to pack her
tuba and get out!

THELMA: But, Reginald——

HARRIS: No—you have pushed me too far. When I married you I
didn't expect to have your mother——

THELMA: (*shouting back at him*) She's not my mother—she's *your*
mother!

HARRIS: (*immediately*) Rubbish!
(*However, he sits down rather suddenly.*)
(*Calmer*) My mother is a . . . tall . . . aristocratic woman, in a
red mac . . . answers to the name of . . .

THELMA: That's your Aunt——

THELMA: ⎱
HARRIS: ⎰ ——Jessica.

(HARRIS *stands up and sits down immediately. His manner is
agitated. He is by now fully dressed.* THELMA *folds the ironing
board and takes it out of the room.* MOTHER *enters, from her
bath, robed or dressed, without the bathing cap, but still hopping
on one foot. She hops across the room.*)

MOTHER: The bulb in the bathroom's gone again. (*She leaves by *the other door.* HARRIS *gets up and goes to the cupboard, extracting his waders.* MOTHER *returns, hopping, carrying a large felt bag.*) I let the water out.

(HARRIS *stuffs the waders back into the cupboard. He moves towards the door, but is most unsettled. He halts, turns and addresses his* MOTHER, *who is now on the wooden chair.*)

HARRIS: (*rather aggressively*) Would you like a cup of tea, Mum?

(*The old lady is startled by the appellation. She looks up, straight ahead, then turns to look at* HARRIS *in a resentful manner.* HARRIS *quails. He turns and is about to leave again when there is a loud knocking on the street door.* MOTHER *continues fiddling with the felt bag, from which, at this moment, she withdraws her tuba.* HARRIS, *with the air of a man more kicked against than kicking, approaches the pile of furniture and begins to take it apart as* MOTHER *puts the tuba to her lips.* MOTHER *plays while* HARRIS *moves the furniture piece by piece into its proper place. Before he has finished,* THELMA *enters with a drink in one hand and a flower vase in the other. She puts them down and helps* HARRIS *with the heavier pieces. The long, low table is placed centrally under the lampshade. The settee goes behind it and a comfortable chair goes either side. This is managed so that* MOTHER *does not have to move from her position on the wooden chair, or desist from playing her jaunty tune, until the last stages, just before the police enter. When they do so—*INSPECTOR FOOT *and* PC HOLMES—*everything is in place, the wooden chair put back against the wall, and the three people seated comfortably.* THELMA *smoking and holding her drink; the tuba out of view, perhaps behind* MOTHER'S *chair. The only surviving oddity is the fruit basket, when the door is finally flung open and* FOOT *charges into the room, right downstage, with* HOLMES *taking up position in a downstage corner and naturally looking a little taken aback.*)

FOOT: What is the meaning of this bizarre spectacle?!!

(*Pause. They all squint about.*)

THELMA: The counterweight fell down and broke. Is that a crime?

(FOOT *clasps both hands behind his back and goes into an aggressive playing-for-time stroll, passing* HOLMES. FOOT *speaks out of the corner of his mouth.*)

FOOT: Got the right house, have you?

HOLMES: Yes, sir.

(FOOT *continues his stroll.* HARRIS *would like to help.*)

MOTHER: (*uncertainly*) Is it all right for me to practise?

(FOOT *ignores her, his eyes darting desperately about until they fix on the table-lamp.* FOOT *stops dead. His head moves slightly along the line of the lampshade, reading the words scrawled on it.*)

FOOT: (*triumphantly*) Reginald William Harris?

HARRIS: Thirty-seven Mafeking Villas.

FOOT: You are addressing a police officer not an envelope. Would you kindly answer my questions in the right order.

HARRIS: I'm sorry.

(FOOT *turns his back on* HARRIS, *denoting a fresh start, and barks.*)

FOOT: Reginald William Harris!

HARRIS: Here.

FOOT: Where do you live?—*you're doing it again!!!*

MOTHER: Who is that man?

FOOT: I am Chief Inspector Foot.

(HARRIS *rises to his feet with a broad enchanted smile.*)

HARRIS: Not Foot of the Y——

FOOT: (*screams*) Silence!

(FOOT *starts travelling again, keeping his agitation almost under control, ignoring* MOTHER'S *murmur.*)

MOTHER: Can I practice now?

(FOOT *arrives at* HOLMES, *and addresses him out of the corner of his mouth.*)

FOOT: Quite sure? You never mentioned the fruit.

HOLMES: (*plaintively*) There was so much else . . .

FOOT: Better have a look round.

HOLMES: Yes, sir.

(THELMA *ignores the convention of the 'aside', raising her voice and her head.*)

THELMA: I'm afraid things are a bit of a mess.

FOOT: (*briskly*) I can't help that. You know what they say—clean knickers every day, you never know when you might be run over. Well it's happened to you on a big scale.

(HARRIS *regains his feet.*)

HARRIS: Just a minute. Have you got a search warrant?
> (HOLMES *pauses*.)

FOOT: Yes.

HARRIS: Can I see it?

FOOT: I can't put my hand to it at the moment.

HARRIS: (*incredulous*) You can't *find* your search warrant!

FOOT: (*smoothly*) I had it about my person when I came in. I may
> have dropped it. Have a look round, Holmes.
> (THELMA *rises to her feet with a broad enchanted smile*.)

THELMA: *Not*——

FOOT: (*screams*) *Be quiet!*
> (THELMA *sits down*. HARRIS *will not*.)

HARRIS: Now look here——

FOOT: Can I see your television licence?
> (HARRIS *freezes with his mouth open. After a long moment he
> closes it*.)

HARRIS: (*vaguely*) Er, it must be about . . . somewhere . . .

FOOT: Good. While you're looking for your television licence,
> Holmes will look for the search warrant.
> (HARRIS *sits down thoughtfully*.)
> (*To* HOLMES) It could have blown about a bit or slipped
> down under the floorboards.

HOLMES: Right, sir. (HOLMES *begins to crawl around the room*.)

MOTHER: Is it all right for me to practise?
> (FOOT *ignores her. He stands looking down smugly at* HARRIS.)

FOOT: Yes, I expect you're wondering what gave you away.

HARRIS: (*wanly*) Was it one of those detector vans?
> (*But* FOOT *is already on the move*.)

FOOT: Well, I'll tell you. It's a simple tale—no hot tips from
> Interpol, no days and nights of keeping watch in the rain, no
> trouser turn-ups hoovered by Forensics or undercover agents
> selling the *Evening News* in Chinatown—no!—just a plain
> ordinary copper on his beat! Yes!—the PC is still the best
> tool the Yard has got!——
> (HOLMES *is behind him, on his hands and knees*.)

HOLMES: Excuse me, sir.

FOOT: (*irritated*) Not in here; *around*.

HOLMES: (*getting to his feet*) Yes, sir. Is this anything, sir? (*He*

hands FOOT *a .22 lead slug which he has found on the floor.*
FOOT *accepts it unheedingly; he is already talking.* HOLMES
leaves the room.)

FOOT: He's not one of your TV heroes, young Holmes—he's just
a young man doing his job and doing it well—sometimes not
seeing his kids—Dean, five, and Sharon, three—for days on
end—often getting home after his wife's asleep and back on
the beat before she wakes—tireless, methodical,
eagle-eyed—always ready with a friendly word for the old lag
crossing the road or sixpence for the old lady trying to go
straight——
(HOLMES *has re-entered the room and has been dogging* FOOT'S
*footsteps, waiting for an opportunity to speak, which he now
deduces, wrongly, has presented itself.*)

HOLMES: To tell you the truth, sir, I'm not absolutely sure what a
search warrant looks like . . .
(*But* FOOT *marches on, round the right-angle of the room, while*
HOLMES *plods stolidly on and out without changing course. As*
FOOT *moves he is weighing and jiggling in his hand the lead slug,
and he has been becoming more aware of its presence there.*)

FOOT: Yes, that's the sort of metal that has brought you to book.
(FOOT *absently examines the object in his hand. He seems
surprised at finding it there.*)
When Holmes got back to the station and described to me
the scene he had witnessed through your window, I realized
he had stumbled on something even bigger than even . . .
(*He tails off, and whirls on them, holding up the metal slug.*) Do
any of you know what this is?
(THELMA *holds up her hand.*)
Well?
(THELMA *gets up and takes the slug out of* FOOT's *hand.*)

THELMA: It's a lead slug from a .22 calibre pistol. Thank you.
(*She tosses the slug into the metal bin wherein it makes the
appropriate sound.*) A hundred and fifty. (*She returns to her
seat.* FOOT *walks over to the metal bin and peers into it. He
bends and takes out a handful of lead slugs and lets them fall
back. He stoops again and comes up with the broken halves of the
porcelain container that had held the slugs and acted as the*

counterweight to the light fitting. He regards the basket of fruit. He drops the debris back into the bin. He addresses himself to THELMA.)

FOOT: It is my duty to tell you that I am not satisfied with your reply.

THELMA: What was the question?

FOOT: That is hardly the point.

THELMA: Ask me another.

FOOT: Very well. Why did it take you so long to answer the door?

THELMA: The furniture was piled up against it.

FOOT: (*sneeringly*) Really? Expecting visitors, Mrs. Harris?

THELMA: On the contrary.

FOOT: In my experience your conduct usually indicates that visitors are expected.

THELMA: I am prepared to defend myself against any logician you care to produce.

FOOT: (*snaps*) Do you often stack the furniture up against the door?

THELMA: Yes. Is that a crime?

FOOT: (*furiously*) Will you stop trying to exploit my professional knowledge for your private ends!—I didn't do twenty years of hard grind to have my brains picked by every ignorant layman who finds out I'm a copper!

(HARRIS *has relapsed into a private brood, from which this outburst rouses him. He has decided to capitulate. He stands up*.)

HARRIS: All right! Can we call off this game of cat and mouse?! I haven't *got* a television licence—I kept meaning to get one but somehow . . .

(FOOT *turns to him*.)

FOOT: Then perhaps you have a diploma from the Royal College of Surgeons.

HARRIS: (*taken aback*) I'm afraid not. I didn't realize they were compulsory.

FOOT: (*without punctuation*) I have reason to believe that within the last hour in this room you performed without anaesthetic an illegal operation on a bald nigger minstrel about five-foot-two or Pakistani and that is only the beginning!

HARRIS: I deny it!

FOOT: Furthermore, that this is a disorderly house!

HARRIS: *That* I admit—Thelma, I've said if before and I'll say it again——

THELMA: (*shouting angrily*) Don't you come that with me!—what with the dancing, the travelling, ironing your shirts, massaging your mother and starting all over every morning, I haven't got time to wipe my nose!

HARRIS: (*equally roused*) *That's* what I want to talk to you about—sniff-sniff—it's a disgusting habit in a woman——

THELMA: (*shouting*) All right—so I've got a cold!—(*Turning to the world, which happens to be in the direction of* FOOT)—Is that a crime?

FOOT: (*hysterically*) I will not warn you again! (*He patrols furiously.*) The disorderliness I was referring to consists of immoral conduct—tarted-up harpies staggering about drunk to the wide, naked men in rubber garments hanging from the lampshade—Have you got a music licence? (*As he passes the gramophone.*)

HARRIS: There is obviously a perfectly logical reason for everything.

FOOT: There is, and I mean to make it stick! What was the nature of this operation? (FOOT *finds himself staring at a line of single greasy footprints leading across the room. He hops along the trail, fascinated, until he reaches the door to* MOTHER's *bath. He turns. Quietly.*) The D.P.P. is going to take a very poor view if you have been offering cut-price amputations to immigrants. (HOLMES *enters excitedly with the ironing board.*)

HOLMES: Sir!

FOOT: That's an ironing board.

HOLMES: (*instantaneously demoralized*) Yes, sir.

FOOT: What we're looking for is a darkie short of a leg or two.

HOLMES: (*retiring*) Right, sir.

MOTHER: Is it all right for me to practise?

FOOT: No, it is not all right! Ministry standards may be lax but we draw the line at Home Surgery to being in the little luxuries of life.

MOTHER: I only practise on the tuba.

FOOT: Tuba, femur, fibula—it takes more than a penchant for

rubber gloves to get a licence nowadays.

MOTHER: The man's quite mad.

FOOT: That's what they said at the station when I sent young Holmes to take a turn down Mafeking Villas, but everything I have heard about events here today convinces me that you are up to your neck in the Crippled Minstrel Caper!

THELMA: Is that a dance?

HARRIS: My wife and I are always on the look-out for novelty numbers. We're prepared to go out on a limb if it's not in a bad taste.

FOOT: (*shouting him down*) Will you kindly stop interrupting while I am about to embark on my exegesis!! (*Pauses, he collects himself.*) The story begins about lunchtime today. The facts appear to be that shortly after two o'clock this afternoon, the talented though handicapped doyen of the Victoria Palace Happy Minstrel Troupe emerged from his dressing-room in blackface, and entered the sanctum of the box-office staff; whereupon, having broken his crutch over the heads of those good ladies, the intrepid uniped made off with the advance takings stuffed into the crocodile boot which, it goes without saying, he had surplus to his conventional requirements.

HARRIS: It must have been a unique moment in the annals of crime.

FOOT: Admittedly, the scene as I have described it is as yet my own reconstruction based on an eye-witness account of the man's flight down nearby Ponsonby Place, where, it is my firm conjecture, Harris, he was driven off by accomplices in a fast car. They might have got away with it had it not been for an elderly lady residing at number seven, who, having nothing to do but sit by her window and watch the world go by, saw flash by in front of her eyes a bizarre and desperate figure. Being herself an old devotee of minstrel shows she recognized him at once for what he was. She was even able to glimpse his broken crutch, the sort of detail that speaks volumes to an experienced detective. By the time she had made her way to her front door, the street was deserted, save for one or two tell-tale coins on the pavement. Nevertheless, it was her report which enabled me to reconstruct the

sequence of events—though I am now inclined to modify the
details inasmuch as the culprit may have been a genuine
coloured man impersonating a minstrel in order to insinuate
himself into the side door to the box office. These are just the
broad strokes. My best man, Sergeant Potter, is at this
moment checking the Victoria Palace end of the case and I
am confidently expecting verification by telephone of my
hypothesis. In any event I think you now understand why I
am here.

HARRIS: No, I'm afraid I'm completely at a loss.

FOOT: Then perhaps you can explain what your car was doing in
Ponsonby Place at twenty-five minutes past two this
afternoon.

HARRIS: So that's it.

FOOT: Exactly. It was bad luck getting that parking ticket,
Harris—one of those twists of fate that have cracked many an
alibi. We traced your car and sent Constable Holmes to take
a look at you.

HARRIS: But we know nothing of this outrage.

FOOT: What were you doing there, right across London?

HARRIS: We went to see an exhibition of surrealistic art at the
Tate Gallery.

FOOT: I must say that in a lifetime of off-the-cuff alibis I have
seldom been moved closer to open derision.

THELMA: Perhaps it would help to explain that my mother-in-law
is a devotee of Maigret.

MOTHER: *Magritte*.

FOOT: I'm afraid I don't follow your drift.

HARRIS: You will when I tell you that she is an accomplished
performer on, and passionate admirer in all its aspects of, the
tuba.

FOOT: Tuba? (*Angrily*.) You are stretching my patience and my
credulity to breaking poi—(*He sees* MOTHER *with the tuba
now on her lap*.)

MOTHER: Can I have a go now?

HARRIS: Hearing that among the canvases on view were several
depicting the instrument of her chief and indeed obsessional
interest, my wife's mother, in law, or rather my mother,

prevailed upon us to take her to the exhibition, which we did, notwithstanding the fact that we could ill afford the time from rehearsing for a professional engagement at the North Circular Dancerama tonight, and to which, I may say, we will shortly have to absent ourselves. (*To* THELMA *without pause*.) Have you taken up your hem?

(THELMA *gasps with dismay and self-reproach and immediately whips off her dress. This leaves her in bra and panties. Her action, since it is not especially remarkable, is not especially remarked upon.* THELMA'*s preoccupation now is to find needle and thread, in which she succeeds quite quickly without leaving the room. However, her chief problem during the ensuing minutes is her lack of a tailor's dummy. She tries draping the dress over various bits of furniture, and tackling the hem, but for one reason or another—the inadequate lighting or the lowness of the chairs, etc.—she is intermittently frustrated until, quite naturally and smoothly, she drapes the dress over* HARRIS, *who simply takes no notice; indeed* THELMA *is reduced to following him on her hands and knees between stitches, and occasionally asking him to keep still. Needless to say, the dress must be sleeveless and full. There has been no pause in the dialogue.*)

Look at her!—with an organized partner I could have reached the top!

FOOT: About your alibi——

MOTHER: It was rubbish.

FOOT: Hah! (*He turns to her.*)

MOTHER: Tubas on fire, tubas stuck to lions and naked women, tubas hanging in the sky—there was one woman with a tuba with a sack over her head as far as I could make out. I doubt he'd ever tried to play one; in fact if you ask me the man must have been some kind of lunatic.

HARRIS: As my mother says, the visit was a disappointment.

THELMA: I must say I have to agree. I don't like to speak slightingly of another artiste, but it just wasn't life-like—I'm not saying it wasn't *good*—well *painted*—but not from life, you know?

FOOT: That has no bearing on the case. Did you see anybody you knew at the exhibition?

MOTHER: I saw Sir Adrian Boult.

FOOT: Would he be prepared to come forward?

HARRIS: You'll have to forgive the old lady. She sees Sir Adrian Boult everywhere.

MOTHER: I saw him in Selfridges.

FOOT: Yes, quite——

MOTHER: He was buying a cushion-cover.

FOOT: (*loudly*) Can we please keep to the point! Which happens to be that after Magritte you apparently returned to your car parked in Ponsonby Place, and drove off at the very moment and from the very spot where the escaping minstrel was last observed, which suggests to me that you may have kept a rendezvous and driven off with him in your car.

HARRIS: That is a monstrous allegation, and, it so happens, a lie.

FOOT: Was there any independent witness who can vouch for that?

MOTHER: Yes—there was that man. He waved at me when we were driving off.

FOOT: Can you describe him?

MOTHER: Yes. He was playing hopscotch on the corner, a man in the loose-fitting striped gaberdine of a convicted felon. He carried a handbag under one arm, and with the other he waved at me with a cricket bat.
(FOOT *reels*.)

FOOT: Would you know him again?

MOTHER: I doubt it. He was wearing dark glasses, and a surgical mask.
(HARRIS *comes forward to restore sanity*.)

HARRIS: My mother is a bit confused, Inspector. It was a tortoise under his arm and he wasn't so much playing hopscotch as one-legged.

THELMA: (*deftly slipping the dress over* HARRIS) A tortoise or a football—he was a young man in a football shirt——

HARRIS: *If* I might just stick my oar in here, he could hardly have been a young man since he had a full white beard, and, if I'm not mistaken, side-whiskers.

THELMA: I don't wish to make an issue of this point, but since it has been raised, the energetic if spasmodic hopping of the man's movements hardly suggests someone in his dotage——

HARRIS: I saw him distinctly through the windscreen——

THELMA: It was, of course, raining at the time——

HARRIS: My windscreen wipers were in order, and working——

FOOT: At any rate, regardless of his age, convictions or hobbies, you claim that this man saw you drive off from Ponsonby Place at 2.25 this afternoon?

HARRIS: I'm afraid not, Inspector. He was blind, sweeping a path before him with a white stick——

THELMA: ——a West Bromwich Albion squad member, swinging an ivory cane—for goodness sake keep still, Reginald—and get up on the table a minute, my back's breaking——

(HARRIS *mounts the low table, thus easing the angle of* THELMA's *back.*)

HARRIS: My wife is a bit confused——

FOOT: So the best witness you can come up with is a blind, white-bearded, one-legged footballer with a tortoise. How do you account for the animal? Was it a seeing-eye tortoise?

HARRIS: I don't see that the tortoise as such requires explanation. Since the fellow was blind he needn't necessarily have known it was a tortoise. He might have picked it up in mistake for some other object such as a lute.

FOOT: His loot?

HARRIS: Or mandolin.

MOTHER: It was, in fact, an alligator handbag.

FOOT: I'm afraid I can't accept these picturesque fantasies. My wife has an alligator handbag and I defy anyone to mistake it for a musical instrument.

THELMA: *STOP!* Don't move! (*They desist.*) I've dropped the needle.

HARRIS: (*looking at his watch*) For God's sake, Thelma——

HARRIS: Help me find it.

(MOTHER *and* FOOT *dutifully get down on their hands and knees with* THELMA. HARRIS *remains standing on the table.* MOTHER *and* FOOT *are head-to-head.*)

MOTHER: Inspector, if the man we saw was blind, who was the other witness?

FOOT: What other witness?

MOTHER: The one who must have told the police about our car being there.

FOOT: My dear lady, you have put your finger on one of the ironies of this extraordinary case. I myself live at number four Ponsonby Place, and it was I, glancing out of an upstairs window, who saw your car pulling away from the kerb.

MOTHER: And yet, you never saw the minstrel?

FOOT: No, the first I knew about it was when I got to the station late this afternoon and read the eye-witness report sent in by the old lady. I must have missed him by seconds, which led me to suspect that he had driven off in your car. I remembered seeing a yellow parking ticket stuck in your windscreen, and the rest was child's play. (*The telephone rings. Getting up and going to it.*) Ah—that will be Sergeant Potter. We shall soon see how my deductions tally with the facts. (FOOT *picks up the phone. The needle search continues.* HARRIS *stands, patient and gowned, on the table.*)

THELMA: Can we have the top light on?

HARRIS: There's no bulb.

THELMA: Get the bulb from the bathroom.

HARRIS: It's gone again.

THELMA: Well, get any bulb!—quickly!

(MOTHER *gets to her one good foot as* FOOT *replaces the phone dumbstruck and shaken. The table-lamp is next to the phone.*)

MOTHER: Could you get the bulb out of that lamp, Inspector?

(FOOT *looks at her unseeingly.*)

The bulb.

(FOOT, *as in a dream, turns to the bulb. His brain has seized up.*)

You'll need a hanky or a glove.

(FOOT *ineffectually pats his pocket.*)

A woollen sock would do.

(FOOT *sits down wearily and slips off one of his shoes and his sock.*)

HARRIS: Is something the matter with your foot, Foot? Inspector, Foot?

(FOOT *thrusts one hand into the woollen sock. With the other he produces from his pocket a pair of heavy dark glasses which he puts on.*)

You wish to inspect your foot, Inspector?

THELMA: *Can we please have some light?*

FOOT: (*quietly*) Yes—of course—forgive me—I get this awful migraine behind the eyes—it's the shock——

MOTHER: What happened, Inspector?

FOOT: It appears that no robbery of the kind I deduced has in fact taken place among the Victoria Palace Happy Minstrel Troupe. Moreover, there is no minstrel troupe, happy or miserable, playing at that theatre or any other. My reconstruction has proved false in every particular, and it is undoubtedly being voiced back at the station that my past success at deductions of a penetrating character has caused me finally to overreach myself in circumstances that could hardly be more humiliating. (*They all sense the enormity of it. HARRIS, however, is unforgiving. He steps down off the table.*)

THELMA: Oh . . . I'm sorry. Is there anything we can do?

MOTHER: I've always found that bananas are very good for headaches.

HARRIS: (*nastily*) So the crime to which you have accused us of being accessories never in fact took place!

FOOT: That is the position, but before you start congratulating yourself, you still have to explain the incredible and suggestive behaviour witnessed by Constable Holmes through your window.

HARRIS: The activities in this room today have broadly speaking been of a mundane and domestic nature bordering on cliché. Police Constable Holmes obviously has an imagination as fervid and treacherous as your own. If he's found a shred of evidence to back it up then get him in here and let's see it.

FOOT: Very well! (*Calls.*) Holmes!

THELMA: Inspector, the bulb, we need the bulb.

(MOTHER *hops over to the wooden chair by the wall, in order to pick it up, though we never see her complete the action.* FOOT'*s attention is still on* HARRIS.)

FOOT: But bear in mind that my error was merely one of interpretation, and whatever did happen in Ponsonby Place this afternoon, your story contains a simple but revealing

mistake which clearly indicates that your so-called alibi is a
tissue of lies.

HARRIS: What do you mean?

FOOT: You claimed that your witness was a blind one-legged
musician.

HARRIS: Roughly speaking.

FOOT: You are obviously unaware that a blind man *cannot stand on
one leg*!

HARRIS: Rubbish!

FOOT: It is impossible to keep one's sense of balance for more
than a few seconds, and if you don't believe me, try it!
(*Black-out as* FOOT *extracts the bulb.*)

HARRIS: I will!

MOTHER: Over here, Inspector.
(*In the darkness, which for these few seconds should be total,*
HARRIS *begins to count, slowly and quietly to himself. But it is*
FOOT's *voice that must be isolated.*)

FOOT: The sudden silence as I enter the canteen will be more than
I can bear . . .

MOTHER: Here we are.

FOOT: The worst of it is, if I'd been up a few minutes earlier I
could have cracked the case and made the arrest before the
station even knew about it.

MOTHER: I'll need the sock.

FOOT: I'd been out with the boys from C Division till dawn, and
left my car outside the house, thinking that I'd move it to a
parking meter before the wardens came round—in my
position one has to set an example, you know. Well, I woke
up late and my migraine was giving me hell and my bowels
were so bad I had to stop half way through shaving, and I
never gave the traffic warden a thought till I glanced out of
the window and saw your car pulling away from the only
parking space in the road. I flung down my razor and rushed
into the street, pausing only to grab my wife's handbag
containing the small change and her parasol to keep off the
rain——

MOTHER: You won't mind if I have my practice now, will you?

FOOT: I got pretty wet because I couldn't unfurl the damned

thing, and I couldn't move fast because in my haste to pull
up my pyjama trousers I put both feet into the same leg. So
after hopping about a bit and nearly dropping the handbag
into various puddles, I just thought to hell with it all and
went back in the house. My wife claimed I'd broken her new
white parasol, and when I finally got out of there I had a
parking ticket. I can tell you it's just been one bitch of a day.

MOTHER: Lights!

THELMA: At last.

(*The central light comes on and the effect is much brighter. The
light has been turned on by* HOLMES, *who stands rooted in the
doorway with his hand still on the switch.*

The row on the table reads from left to right:

(*1*) MOTHER, *standing on her good foot only, on the wooden
chair which is placed on the table; a woollen sock on one hand;
playing the tuba.*

(*2*) *Lightshade, slowly descending towards the table.*

(*3*) FOOT, *with one bare foot, sunglasses, eating banana.*

(*4*) *Fruit basket, slowly ascending.*

(*5*) HARRIS, *gowned, blindfolded with a cushion cover over his
head, arms outstretched, on one leg, counting.*

THELMA, *in underwear, crawling around the table, scanning the
floor and sniffing.* HOLMES *recoils into paralysis.*)

FOOT: Well, Constable, I think you owe us all an explanation.

(*The lampshade descends inexorably as the music continues to
play; when it touches the table-top, there is no more light.
Alternatively, the lampshade could disappear down the horn of
the tuba.*)

DIRTY LINEN
A play in one act

To Ed Berman

Dirty Linen was supposed to be a play to celebrate Ed Berman's British naturalization, but it went off in a different direction— *New-Found-Land* was then written to re-introduce the American Connection.

Ed Berman, an expatriate American, founded Inter-Action, a charitable trust aiming to stimulate community involvement in the arts, in 1968. He now works as the Artistic Director of Inter-Action Productions (including the Ambiance Lunch-Hour Theatre Club, the Almost Free Theatre, the Fun Art Bus and the Dogg's Troupe). Not coincidentally like the American seeking British naturalization in *New-Found-Land* and like other members of Inter-Action's co-operative, he divides his time between the production company and work in schools, youth clubs, mental hospitals, community centres, playgrounds, remand homes and the streets. Most of his time is now spent as Programme Director of Inter-Action Trust, creating new community arts and action projects such as City Farms 1 in Kentish Town, and youth employment programmes. He still manages to direct some ten plays a year, mainly for children's and community theatre, and to perform in two hundred-odd shows. Ed Berman became a British subject on 5th April 1976, the date of the first public showing of *Dirty Linen* and *New-Found-Land*.

TOM STOPPARD
1976

Characters

MADDIE
COCKLEBURY-SMYTHE, M.P.
MCTEAZLE, M.P.
CHAMBERLAIN, M.P.
WITHENSHAW, M.P. (the CHAIRMAN)
MRS. EBURY, M.P.
FRENCH, M.P.
HOME SECRETARY

The first performances of *Dirty Linen* and *New-Found-Land* were an Ambiance Lunch-Hour Theatre Club presentation at Inter-Action's Almost Free Theatre, Rupert Street, London W1, on 6th April 1976. The cast was as follows:

Dirty Linen

MADDIE	Luan Peters
COCKLEBURY-SMYTHE, M.P.	Edward de Souza
MCTEAZLE, M.P.	Benjamin Whitrow
CHAMBERLAIN, M.P.	Malcolm Ingram
WITHENSHAW, M.P. (the CHAIRMAN)	Peter Bowles
MRS. EBURY, M.P.	Christine Ozanne
FRENCH, M.P.	Richard O'Callaghan
HOME SECRETARY	Derek Ensor

New-Found-Land

ARTHUR	Stephen Moore
BERNARD	Richard Goolden

Directed by Ed Berman
Designed by Gabriella Falk
Production Management and lighting by Suresa Galbraith
Administration by Martin Turner
Stage Management by Robin Hornibrook and Brenda Lipson
Wardrobe by Carol Betera

The plays transferred to the Arts Theatre on 16th June 1976 with the following cast changes:

MCTEAZLE, M.P.	Frederick Treves
FRENCH, M.P.	Jonathan Elsom

An overspill meeting room for House of Commons business in the tower of Big Ben. A committee table with chairs for everybody; separate table with good slammable drawers for MADDIE; *large blackboard on easel; shelves of files and books, with portable steps; and two doors.*

Ultimately the characters will be seated in the following order, left to right from the audience's point of view: FRENCH, CHAMBERLAIN, COCKLEBURY-SMYTHE, WITHENSHAW (*centre*), MRS. EBURY, MCTEAZLE, *and* MADDIE *at separate desk.*

The room is empty. MADDIE *puts her head round the door cautiously, enters in street coat and carrying a small classy looking bag from a classy lingerie shop, and a handbag. The room is unfamiliar to her. She hangs up her coat on a coat/hat/umbrella stand which is just inside the door, walks to the desk, and after a moment's hesitation she takes a pair of silk, lace-trimmed French knickers out of the bag and puts them on.*

MADDIE *finishes putting on her knickers and drops her skirt. The knickers ought to be remembered for their colour—perhaps white silk with red lace trimmings.*

MADDIE *is now wearing a low cut, sleeveless blouse, buttoned insecurely down the front; a wrap-round skirt, quite short; underneath, suspenders not tights, and a waist-slip which is also pretty, silk and lace, with a slit.*

From her bag she takes a notebook and a pencil and puts them on the desk. There are glasses and a carafe on the large table. She picks up the lingerie bag and looks around for a waste-paper basket. Finding none, she leaves by the other door, bag in hand. The first door is now opened by MCTEAZLE *who holds it open for* COCKLEBURY-SMYTHE.

COCKLEBURY-SMYTHE (*entering*): Toujours la politesse.
MCTEAZLE (*closing the door*): Noblesse oblige.

(*They each carry several newspapers, a whole crop of the day's papers and the Sundays, which they dump on the big table. They doff their bowler hats and attempt to put them on the same peg.*)

Mea culpa. (*Courteously.*)

COCKLEBURY-SMYTHE: Après vous.

(MCTEAZLE *signals that* COCKLEBURY-SMYTHE *should hang up his hat first. They put their brollies in the umbrella stand.* COCKLEBURY-SMYTHE *sits down.*)

J'y suis, j'y reste. (*He opens the* Daily Mail.) Quel dommage.

MCTEAZLE (*sitting down*): Le mot juste.

COCKLEBURY-SMYTHE: C'est la vie. Che sera sera. (*He throws the paper aside.*)

(MCTEAZLE *picks up the* Daily Mirror *and turns to page 3 which features a glamour picture, not particularly revealing.*)

MCTEAZLE: Ooh la-la! (*Then he recovers his dignity. Deprecatingly.* Vox populi . . . plus ça change, plus c'est la même chose. (*He throws the paper aside and picks up the* Guardian.)

COCKLEBURY-SMYTHE: De gustibus non est disputandum.

(*Pause.*)

MCTEAZLE (*hesitantly*): A propos . . . entre nous . . . vis-à-vis le Coq d'Or.

COCKLEBURY-SMYTHE: Ah, le Coq d'Or . . .

MCTEAZLE: Faux pas, hein?

COCKLEBURY-SMYTHE: Bloody awkward though. Pardon my French.

(MADDIE *re-enters with a waste-paper basket.* MCTEAZLE *does not see her as he is engrossed in the* Guardian. COCKLEBURY-SMYTHE *sees her but registers nothing.*)

Honi soit qui mal y pense.

(*On which, without pausing, he produces from an inside pocket a pair of French knickers and hands them to* MADDIE *as she crosses to her desk collecting them urbanely.*)

Ergo nil desperandum.

(COCKLEBURY-SMYTHE *picks up his copy of the* Daily Mirror *and turns to the pin-up on page 3. He makes a wordless noise appropriate to male approval of female pulchritude. This coincides with* MADDIE *bending over, showing cleavage, to put*

*the knickers into a drawer of her desk. This moment of the man
reacting to the pin-up photograph, and the coincidental image
of* MADDIE *in a pin-up pose is something which is to be repeated
several times, so for brevity's sake it will be hereafter
symbolized by the expletive 'Strewth!' It must be marked
distinctly; a momentary freeze on stage, and probably a flash
of light like a camera flash.* MADDIE *should look straight out at
the audience for that moment.*)

Strewth!

(*After the freeze* MCTEAZLE *sees* MADDIE.)

MCTEAZLE: Good afternoon. (*He stands up.*) I am Mr. McTeazle
and you are . . . ?

MADDIE: Miss Gotobed.

MCTEAZLE: Miss Gotobed. And this is Mr. Cocklebury-Smythe.

COCKLEBURY-SMYTHE: How do you do?

MADDIE: Hello.

COCKLEBURY-SMYTHE: So you are going to be our clerk.

MADDIE: Yes.

COCKLEBURY-SMYTHE: May I be the first to welcome you to
Room 3b. You will find the working conditions primitive,
the hours antisocial, the amenities non-existent and the
catering beneath contempt. On top of that the people are for
the most part very very very boring, with interests either so
generalized as to mimic wholesale ignorance or so particular
as to be lunatic obsessions. Their level of conversation
would pass without comment in the lavatory of a mixed
comprehensive and the lavatories, by the way, are few and
far between.

MADDIE: It has always been my ambition to work in the House
of Commons.

(*Sound of Big Ben chiming the half hour.*)

COCKLEBURY-SMYTHE: Mine has always been the House of Lords.
But then perhaps I have not been willing to make the same
sacrifices you have.

MCTEAZLE: Have you had to make sacrifices Miss Gotobed? Not
too arduous I hope?

MADDIE: It was hard work but I enjoyed the challenge.

COCKLEBURY-SMYTHE (*quickly*): Yes . . . yes, the P.M. offered me

a life peerage, for services which he said he would let me
know more about in due course if I were interested. 'I hear
you're a keen gardener, Cockie,' he said, 'we can call it
services to conservation.' 'Not me, Rollo,' I said, 'all I use
it for is a little topiary in the summer.' 'Services to sport,'
he said, 'ignorant fool.' 'No, no, Rollo,' I said, 'I really have
no interests of any kind.' 'That will be services to the arts,'
he said. 'Stop making such a fuss—do you want a life
peerage or don't you?' 'No I don't,' I said to him. 'What
with only a couple of bachelor cousins in line ahead, one of
whom is an amateur parachutist and the other a seamstress
in the Merchant Navy, I prefer to hang on for a chance of
the real thing.' He said to me: 'My dear Cockie, life peers
are the real thing nowadays.' 'Oh no they're not, Rollo,' I
said. 'That's just the kind of confusion you set up in people's
minds by calling them Lord This and Lord That, pour
encourager hoi polloi. *They* think they're lords—they skip
off home and feed the budgerigar saying to themselves, my
golly gorblimey, I'm a lord! They'd be just as happy if you
suddenly told them they were all sheiks. They'd put the
Desert Song on the gramophone and clap their hands when
they wanted their cocoa. Now *you'd* know they're not really
sheiks and I'd know they're not really sheiks, and God help
them if they ever showed up east of Suez in their appalling
pullovers with Sheik Shuttleworth stencilled on their airline
bags—no, my dear Rollo,' I said, 'I'll be a real peer or not
at all.' 'Now look here, Cockie,' he said to me, 'if they
weren't real peers they wouldn't be in the House of Lords
would they?—that's logic.' 'If that's logic,' I said, 'you can
turn a regimental goat into a Lieutenant Colonel by
electing it to the United Services Club.' 'That's an
interesting point, Cockie,' he said. 'It could explain a lot of
my problems.' Do you suppose we've got the wrong day?
(*He takes out a pocket diary and consults it.*) Oh yes—
Select Committee, House of Commons—take L.P. . . . take
L.P. . . . ? What L.P.?

MADDIE: It is the right day. I didn't get a wink of sleep all last
night.

COCKLEBURY-SMYTHE (*mutters*): L.P. . . .

MADDIE: It's not every girl who gets advancement from the Home Office typing pool.

MCTEAZLE: I expect it's not every girl who proves herself as you have done, Miss Gotobed. Do you use Gregg's or do you favour the Pitman method?

MADDIE: I'm on the pill.

(*Small pause.* MCTEAZLE *is expressionless.*)

MCTEAZLE: Perhaps this might be an opportunity for me to explain to you the nature of the duties expected of a secretary/clerk attached to a Select Committee, duties which for one reason or another you may have got confused in your mind.

COCKLEBURY-SMYTHE (*suddenly*): Lace panties. Sorry.

MCTEAZLE: Now, this is a meeting of a Select Committee of Members of Parliament to report on moral standards in the House—not in the House literally, or rather, in the House literally but also, and for the most part, outside the House too.

MADDIE: In the car park?

MCTEAZLE: Not literally in the car park—or rather in the car park too, yes, but also—don't try to take in more than you can. Now, this is a continuation of a Select Committee set up during the last session of Parliament, though at that time the membership of the Committee was different. A Select Committee must be reconvened with each new session of Parliament, and it is this reconstituted Committee which is about to begin sitting to report on rumours of sexual promiscuity by certain unspecified Members which, if substantiated, might tend to bring into disrepute the House of Commons and possibly the Lords and one or two government departments including Social Security, Environment, Defence, Health, Agriculture and even, I'm sorry to say, the Milk Marketing Board.

MADDIE: Why's that?

MCTEAZLE: Because I have the honour to be on that Board and I think I can say without fear of contradiction that the M.M.B. has an unrivalled record of freedom from suggestions of

being a sexual free-for-all, and furthermore we are now
getting yoghurt and single and double cream to every
corner of——

MADDIE: Actually what I meant was, why would it bring them
into disrepute?

MCTEAZLE: Because the country by and large looks to its elected
representatives to set a moral standard . . .

MADDIE: No it doesn't——

MCTEAZLE (*smoothly*): No it doesn't—you're quite right. Then
it's because the authority of the—er—authorities is under-
mined by losing the respect of——

MADDIE: I don't think people care.

MCTEAZLE: No, people don't care—of course they don't. In which
case I think it is fair to say that this Committee owes its
existence to the determination of the Prime Minister to keep
his House in order, whatever the cost in public ridicule,
whatever the consequence to people in high places, and to
the fact that the newspapers got wind of what was going on.
It is unfortunate that the well known restraint and sense of
higher purpose which characterizes the British press—a
restraint which would have treated with utter contempt
stories of garter-snapping by a few M.P.s—gave way
completely at the rumour that they were all snapping the
same garter. You may know, if you are a student of the
press, or if you have at any time in the last few weeks
passed within six feet of a newspaper, that there is no phrase
as certain to make a British sub-editor lose his sense of
proportion as the phrase 'Mystery Woman'. This Committee
was set up at the time when the good name of no fewer than
21 Members of Parliament was said to have been com-
promised. Since then rumour has fed on rumour and we
face the possibility that a sexual swathe has passed through
Westminster claiming the reputations of, to put no finer
point upon it, 119 Members. Someone is going through the
ranks like a lawn-mower in knickers. Well, I need hardly
say—(*he is taking papers out of his brief case*)—that we as a
Committee are working in a sensitive area, one which
demands great tact on all our parts—(MCTEAZLE *produces*

from his brief case a pair of knickers and hands them to
MADDIE)—your own not excluded.
(MADDIE *collects the knickers urbanely and puts them in her
knicker drawer; she has changed her position however and has
to practically sprawl across the desk to do this, thus showing
leg as well as cleavage. Simultaneously* COCKLEBURY-SMYTHE
has discovered a pin-up picture in the Daily Mail, *or any other
appropriate paper except the* Sun.)

COCKLEBURY-SMYTHE: Strewth!
(*After the freeze there seems to be nothing to occupy the two
men.* MADDIE *collects herself and sits demurely on her desk. The
two men get up and move around.*)
Well, this is getting us nowhere. Where is everybody?
(*In the following section, the italicized words are said privately
to* MADDIE *with no change of tone or volume while the other is
at the extreme of his perambulation.*)
Are we going to have a quorum? You may not be familiar
with the term quorum incidentally *if anyone asks you where
you had dinner last night* it's a Latin word meaning 'of
which or of whom'. . . .

MCTEAZLE: Quite simply, it's the smallest number of members of
a committee necessary to constitute the said committee, for
example, say you were *nowhere near the Coq d'Or on
Saturday night* then the smallest number of members
without which a quorum can't be said to be a quorum——

COCKLEBURY-SMYTHE: A quorum is nothing more or less than the
largest minimum specified number of members being that
proportion of the whole committee, let us say three or four
get Coq d'Or Sunday night completely invalid without them.
Got it?

MCTEAZLE: It's not as complicated as it sounds.

MADDIE: Is it a specified number of members of a committee
whose presence—God bless them—is necessary for the valid
transaction of business by that committee?

MCTEAZLE: Yes . . . yes, that is pretty well what a quorum is. I
can see, Miss Gotobed, that there is more to you than your
name suggests—by which I mean (*trying to accelerate out of
trouble*) that you don't spend all your time flat on your back

—or your front—your side, flat on your side, sleeping, fast asleep, when you could be doing your homework instead of living up to your name, which you don't, that's my point.
(COCKLEBURY-SMYTHE *has been standing like stone, his glazed eyes absently fixed on* MADDIE'*s cleavage.*)

COCKLEBURY-SMYTHE: McTeazle, why don't you go and see if you can raise those great tits—boobs—those boobies, absolute tits, don't you agree, Malcolm and Douglas—though good men as well, of course, useful chaps, very decent, first rate, two of the best, Malcolm and Douglas, why don't you have a quick poke, peek, in the Members' Bra—or the cafeteria, they're probably guzzling coffee and Swedish panties, (MADDIE *has crossed her legs*) Danish, I'll tell you what, why don't you go and see if you can raise Malcolm and Douglas—(*to* MADDIE)—sometimes there are more of these committees trying to meet than there are rooms for them to meet in—that's why we're up here in the tower instead of one of those nice rooms on the Committee Floor with the green leather chairs, though I expect you've spent a lot of time on the Floor, Miss Gotobed, by which I mean, of course, the Committee Bed, Floor—(*getting hysterical*)— McTeazle the Division Bell will go before we even get started and then we'll all have to go off and vote on some beastly amendment to make anyone who buys his own council house a life bishop with the right to wear a nightie on his head, mitre on his head. My God, I could do with a drink——

MCTEAZLE: You go then. No, I'll go. I'll tell you what, Miss Gotobed, why don't you come with me, I'll show you round the lavatories, round the House, show you the Chamber, the lavatories——

COCKLEBURY-SMYTHE: She doesn't want to go trudging round the House inspecting the toilets like a deputation from the Water Board. Let the poor girl alone—she didn't get a wink of sleep all night.
(*He ushers* MCTEAZLE *out and closes the door. He turns and addresses* MADDIE *immediately. In the following speech the italicized words coincide with* MCTEAZLE'*s brief re-appearance to*

take his bowler hat off the hatstand.)

Maddie my dear, you look even more ravishing this
morning than *the smallest specified number of members of that
committee of which* we will have to be very very careful—it
is a cruel irony that our carefree little friendship, which
is as innocent and pure as the first driven snowdrop of
spring, is in danger of being trampled by the hobnailed
hue-and-cry over these absurd rumours of unbuttoned
behaviour in and out of both trousers of Parliament—I think
I can say, and say with confidence, that when the smoke has
cleared from the Augean stables, the little flame of our love
will still be something no one else can hold a candle to so
long as we can keep our heads down. In other words, my
darling girl, if anyone were to ask you where you had
lunch on Friday, breakfast on Saturday or dinner on
Sunday, best thing is to forget Crockford's, Claridges and
the Coq d'Or.

MADDIE (*concentrating*): Crockford's—Claridges—the Coq d'Or.

COCKLEBURY-SMYTHE: Forget—forget.

MADDIE: Forget. Forget Crockford's, Claridges, Coq d'Or.
Forget Crockford's, Claridges, Coq d'Or. (*To herself.*)
Forget Crockford's, Claridges, Coq d'Or. Forget Crock-
ford's, Claridges, Coq d'Or.

(COCKLEBURY-SMYTHE *sees that this is achieving the opposite.*)

COCKLEBURY-SMYTHE: All right—tell you what—say you had
breakfast at Claridges, *lunch* at the Coq d'Or, and had
dinner at Crockford's. Meanwhile I'll stick to——

MADDIE (*concentrating harder than ever*): Claridges, Coq d'Or,
Crockford's. Forget Crockford's, Claridges, Coq d'Or.
Remember Claridges, Coq d'Or, Crockford's. Remember
Claridges, Coq d'Or, Crockford's. Claridges, Coq d'Or,
Crockford's, Claridges, Coq d'Or, Crockford's.

COCKLEBURY-SMYTHE: But not with me.

MADDIE: Not with you. Not with Cockie at Claridges, Coq d'Or,
Crockford's. Never at Claridges, Coq d'Or, Crockford's
with Cockie. Never at Claridges, Coq d'Or, Crockford's
with Cockie.

(*Her concentration doesn't imply slowness: she is fast, eager,*

*breathless, very good at tongue twisters. Her whole attitude in
the play is one of innocent, eager willingness to please.*
COCKLEBURY-SMYTHE *sees that he is going about this the wrong
way.*)

COCKLEBURY-SMYTHE: Wait a minute. (*Rapidly.*) The best thing
is forget Claridges, Crockford's and the Coq d'Or altogether.

MADDIE: Right. Forget Claridges, Crockford's, Coq d'Or—
forget Claridges, Crockford's, Coq d'Or——

COCKLEBURY-SMYTHE: And if anyone asks you where you had
lunch on Friday, breakfast on Saturday and dinner last
night, when you were with me, tell them where you had
dinner on Friday, lunch on Saturday and breakfast
yesterday.

MADDIE: Right! (*Pause. She closes her eyes with concentration.*)
(*Rapidly.*) The Green Cockatoo, the Crooked Clock, the
Crock of Gold—and Box Hill.

COCKLEBURY-SMYTHE: Box Hill?

MADDIE: To see the moon come up—forget Crockford's,
Claridges, Coq d'Or—remember the Crock of Gold, Box
Hill, the Crooked Clock and the Green Door——

COCKLEBURY-SMYTHE: Cockatoo——

MADDIE: Cockatoo. Crock of Gold, Crooked Clock, Green
Cockatoo and Box Hill. When was this?

COCKLEBURY-SMYTHE: When you were really with me.

MADDIE: Right. With Cockie at the Green Cockatoo——

COCKLEBURY-SMYTHE: No *not* with Cockie at the Green Cockatoo.

MADDIE: —not with Cockie at the Green Cockatoo, the Old
Cook, the Crooked Grin, Gamages and Box Hill.

COCKLEBURY-SMYTHE (*wildly*): No—look. The simplest thing is to
forget, Claridges, the Old Boot, the Golden *quorum can be
any number agreed upon by*——
(*This is because* MCTEAZLE *is back.*)

MCTEAZLE: Douglas is on his way back. (*Hanging up his hat.*)

COCKLEBURY-SMYTHE: I've got to have a drink.
(*He leaves, forgetting his bowler hat, as* MCTEAZLE *closes the
door.* MCTEAZLE *starts speaking at once. The italicized words
correspond to* COCKLEBURY-SMYTHE's *momentary reappearances,
in the first case to take a bowler hat off the hatstand and in*

the second case to change hats because he has taken out
MCTEAZLE'*s hat the first time.*)

MCTEAZLE: Maddie*ning the way one is kept waiting for* ours is a
very tricky position, my dear. In normal times one can
count on chaps being quite sympathetic to the sight of a
Member of Parliament having dinner with a lovely young
woman in some out-of-the-way nook—it could be a case of
constituency business, they're not necessarily screw-*oo-ooge
is, I think you'll find, not in 'David Copperfield' at all, still
less in 'The Old Curiosity Sho*'-cking though it is, the sight
of a Member of Parliament having some out-of-the-way
nookie with a lovely young woman might well be a case of a
genuine love match destined to take root and pass through
ever more respectable stages—the first shy tentative dinner
party in a basement flat in Pembridge Crescent for a few
trusted friends—Caxton Hall—and a real friendship with
the stepchildren—people are normally inclined to give one
the benefit of the doubt. But the tragedy is, as our luck
would have it, that our gemlike love which burns so true
and pure and has brought such a golden light into our
lives, could well become confused with a network of grubby
affairs between men who should know better and some bit
of fluff from the filing department—so I suggest, my darling,
if any one were to enquire where you may or may not have
spent Friday night or indeed Saturday lunch time or Sunday
tea time, forget Charing Cross, the Coq d'Or and the
Golden Ox.

MADDIE: Charing Cross, Coq d'Or, Golden Ox. Charing Cross,
Coq d'Or, Golden Ox. Charing Cross, Old Door, and the
Golden Cock——

MCTEAZLE:—Ox——

MADDIE: Ox.

MCTEAZLE: The Coq d'Or and the Golden Ox. Not the Golden
Cock and the Old Door.

MADDIE: Not the Golden Cock and the Old Door but the
Golden Ox and the Coq d'Or.

MCTEAZLE: And don't forget: Charing Cross.

MADDIE: Don't forget Charing Cross.

MCTEAZLE: I mean *forget* Charing Cross.

MADDIE: Forget Charing Cross——

MCTEAZLE: Plucky girl——

MADDIE: Plucky girl—Charing Cross—Olden cocks.

MCTEAZLE: But not with me.

MADDIE: Not with Jock at the Old Cock——

MCTEAZLE: Door. (*This is because the door has opened.*)

MADDIE: Old Coq d'Or—not with Jock.

> (CHAMBERLAIN *has entered.*)

MCTEAZLE (*hurriedly*): Hello, Douglas.

> (CHAMBERLAIN *is repellently full of zest and heartiness. He also carries an armful of papers which he dumps on the table. He treats* MADDIE *with open, crude lechery.*)

CHAMBERLAIN: Hello!

MCTEAZLE: This is Mr. Chamberlain. Miss Gotobed is going to be our clerk.

> (CHAMBERLAIN *advances on* MADDIE *who backs off behind her desk and starts opening drawers to look busy.*)

CHAMBERLAIN: What?!—that luscious creature is our clerk! Impossible! Where's her moustache? Her dandruff? Her striped pants?

> (MADDIE *reflexively slams shut her knicker drawer.*)

What an uncommonly comely clerk you are! My name's Douglas. I hope you don't mind me saying that you're a lovely girl—I don't mind telling you that if I wasn't married to a wonderful girl myself with two fine youngsters down in Dorking and an au pair to complicate my life, I'd be after you and no mistake,

> (*During the rest of this speech,* MADDIE *pushes past* CHAMBERLAIN, *goes over to her coat and takes a copy of the* Sun *from her pocket. She returns towards her desk.*)

my goodness yes, it would be private coaching in a little French restaurant somewhere, a few hints on parliamentary procedure over the boeuf bourgignon, and then off in the Volvo while I mutter sweet definitions in your ear and test your elastic with the moon coming up over Box Hill.

> (*As* MADDIE *passes the steps, he gooses her so thoroughly that she goes straight up them, still holding the* Sun. CHAMBERLAIN

slaps a sheet of paper on her desk.)

Have you an order of business? (*He turns aside.*) Well, well, here we are without a quorum and I thought I was going to be late. (*To* MADDIE.) You'll know, of course, that a quorum is a specified number of members of a committee whose presence—God bless them—is necessary for the valid transaction of business by that committee—got it? Good.

(CHAMBERLAIN *opens the* Daily Mirror *to the pin-up page.* MCTEAZLE *helps* MADDIE *down the steps; her skirt comes away in his hand.*)

Strewth!

(*After the freeze* MCTEAZLE *tries to shove the skirt at* MADDIE *who has sat down primly behind her desk, but* COCKLEBURY-SMYTHE *enters so* MCTEAZLE *sits on the skirt.*)

COCKLEBURY-SMYTHE: Do we have a quorum?

CHAMBERLAIN: Hello, Cocklebury-Smythe.

COCKLEBURY-SMYTHE: So glad you could come, Chamberlain. You know Miss Gotobed?

CHAMBERLAIN (*over-reacts*): No.

COCKLEBURY-SMYTHE: Mr. Chamberlain—Miss Gotobed.

CHAMBERLAIN: I meant I didn't *know* her.

COCKLEBURY-SMYTHE: Of course you don't know her. All we need now is our Chairman. I wish he'd get his clogs on.

(*The door opens and* WITHENSHAW, *the Chairman, enters. He is a Lancastrian. He also carries newspapers and a brief case.*)

WITHENSHAW: There's trouble in t'*Mail.*

COCKLEBURY-SMYTHE: Mill.

WITHENSHAW: *Mail.* (*He throws the papers and his brief case on to the table.*)

COCKLEBURY-SMYTHE: Oh yes.

WITHENSHAW (*at* MADDIE): And who have we got here?

MADDIE: I'm the clerk. Miss Gotobed.

WITHENSHAW: And I'm Malcolm Withyou! (*He laughs uproariously.*) Malcolm Withyou!—'ee you've got to be quick—Malcolm Withenshaw, Chairman of Select Committee on Promiscuity in High Places. Have you got an order of business? (*He snatches Chamberlain's piece of paper off her desk.*) 'Forget Golden Goose, Selfridges——'

(MADDIE *snatches the paper out of his hand and hands him in the same movement a sealed envelope from her bag.*)

MADDIE: This is for you.

WITHENSHAW (*generally*): Before I saw bloody paper I was going to congratulate you all on a clean bill of health. You can't have a committee washing dirty linen in the corridors of power unless every member is above suspicion. (*On which he produces from the envelope a large pair of Y-front pants which he immediately shoves back into the envelope.*) The wheres and Y-fronts, the whys and wherefores of this Committee are clear to you all. Our presence here today is testimony to the trust the House has in us as individuals and that includes you Maddiemoiselle. (*To* MADDIE.) Though you have been completely unaware of it your private life has been under intense scrutiny by top man in Security Service, a man so senior that I can't even tell you his name——

MADDIE: Fanshawe.

WITHENSHAW: Fanshawe—and you passed test. (*He has been looking around for a place to put his pants, and decides on* MADDIE'*s desk drawer.*) Indeed the fact that you've jumped over heads of many senior clerks indicates that you passed with flying knickers. (*This slip of the tongue is because he has discovered the knickers in the drawer; he drops them back and slams the drawer.*) So it is all the more unfortunate to find stuff in the press like following: Thank you Cockie.

(COCKLEBURY-SMYTHE *reads from the* Daily Mail.)

COCKLEBURY-SMYTHE: 'On the day the Select Committee on Moral Standards in Public Life is due to reconvene I ask— was it wise for one of the members to be seen holding hands under the table with a staggeringly voluptuous, titian-haired green eyed beauty in a West End restaurant at the weekend? And if so, was it modest to choose the Coq d'Or?'

(*Meanwhile,* WITHENSHAW *has finished scribbling a note.*)

WITHENSHAW: Right. Bloody smart alec. Still, least said soonest mended. (*He tosses the note, which is on white paper the size of an old-fashioned £5 note, on to* MADDIE'*s desk.*) Now then, I think you have received prior copies of my draft report, and we'll go through it paragraph by paragraph in the usual way——

MCTEAZLE: Excuse me. Are we now in session?

WITHENSHAW: What's quorum Miss Gotobed?

MADDIE: Is it a specified number of——

CHAMBERLAIN (*hurriedly*): Four, Mr. Chairman.

WITHENSHAW: Then we'll kick off. Get your pencil out, lass.

MADDIE: Do I have to write down what you say?

WITHENSHAW: I can see you know your way around these committees, Miss Gotobed. You do speedwriting I suppose?

MADDIE: Yes, if I'm given enough time.

WITHENSHAW: That's all right. You just tell us if we're going too fast. Here's a copy of my draft report, and appendix A, B, C, and D . . . (*He is giving her these things out of his brief case, into which he puts the envelope containing his pants.*) . . . so it'll just be a matter of keeping a record of amendments, if any.

COCKLEBURY-SMYTHE: Excuse me, Withenshaw, but isn't it rather unusual to have a report by a Select Committee before the Committee has had the advantage of considering the evidence?

WITHENSHAW: Yes, it is unusual, Mr. Cocklebury-Smythe, but this is an unusual situation. As you know sexual immorality unites all parties. This Committee isn't here to play politics. You'll have your chance with amendments, for which you can have all the time in the world. In fact the P.M. insists on it—he doesn't want us to rush into print, he wants a thorough job which he can present to the House the day before the Queen's Silver Jubilee, along with trade figures.

MCTEAZLE: Isn't that going to cause rather a lot of flak in the 1922 Committee and the P.L.P.?

WITHENSHAW: Very likely, but by that time, I'm happy to say, I'm going to be well out of it in the Lords—life peerage for services to arts.

COCKLEBURY-SMYTHE: Services to the *arts*?

WITHENSHAW: I'll have you bloody know Mrs. Withenshaw and I have personally donated the Botticelli-style painted ceiling in the Free Church Assembly Hall. I've bought and paid for more naked bums than you've had hot dinners.

COCKLEBURY-SMYTHE: I'm glad to say I've had more hot dinners.

WITHENSHAW: I speak sub-cathedral of course—no one else
knows except Mrs. Withenshaw, and I shouldn't have told
her—she's taken to wearing white gloves up to elbows to
greyhounds. Anyway, what the P.M. wants is a unanimous
report, if possible declaring—(*as if remembering*)—that there
is no evidence that Members have engaged in scandalous
conduct above the national average, or alternatively that
they may have done in isolated cases, but are we going to
judge grown responsible men in this day and age by the
standards of Mrs. Grundy—whoever she may be—is it that
old bag from Chorleywood South?

COCKLEBURY-SMYTHE: But what's the report based on if we
aren't going to call any witnesses?

WITHENSHAW: What witnesses do you want to call?

COCKLEBURY-SMYTHE: Well . . . I personally wouldn't wish to
call any——

MCTEAZLE: Hear, hear!

CHAMBERLAIN: Absolutely!

COCKLEBURY-SMYTHE: I've no time for stool pigeons admittedly——

MCTEAZLE: Hear, hear!

CHAMBERLAIN: Absolutely!

WITHENSHAW: There aren't any bloody witnesses. No one has
seen anything. It's all bloody innuendo to sell newspapers
in slack period.

ALL: Hear, hear!

WITHENSHAW: What with all the giant killers knocked out of
Cup, and Ceylon versus Bangladesh—I don't call *that* a
bloody test match—the papers naturally resort to sticking
their noses into upper reaches of top drawers looking for
hankie panties, etcetera. . . .

ALL: Hear, hear!

WITHENSHAW: I tell you, if those bloody pandas had got stuck in
and produced a cuddly black and white nipper for London
Zoo, it wouldn't be *us* in spotlight——

ALL: Hear, hear!

WITHENSHAW: Or Mark and Anne for that matter.

COCKLEBURY-SMYTHE: Steady on, Malcolm.

WITHENSHAW: I don't mean it would be black and white.

COCKLEBURY-SMYTHE: Can we move on?

WITHENSHAW: I was just making the point that there's nothing
    to witness just because a member of this Committee is so
    bowed down with the burden of representing his con-
    stituency, while trying to make a decent living in his spare
    time, that he has to take his—homework—to lunch in a
    West End restaurant.

ALL: Hear, hear!

CHAMBERLAIN: *Or* to dinner—pilloried for a beef stew in a
    modest eating house with a professional appointment, for
    all anyone knows a vicar's daughter worried sick about the
    new motorway.

MCTEAZLE: Any cynic can make it look like a hole-in-the-corner
    affair in an out-of-the-way nook like the Coq d'Or quite
    probably is, many of these French places are——

COCKLEBURY-SMYTHE: Nor was it a case of holding hands under
    the table.

ALL: Hear, hear!

COCKLEBURY-SMYTHE: Probably she was passing him the money
    under the table, or vice versa.

MCTEAZLE: The table under the money——

COCKLEBURY-SMYTHE: —him passing *her* the money under the
    table—probably a financially embarrassed lobbyist for
    sexual equality taking an M.P. to a working dinner.

MCTEAZLE: Women's lib——

WITHENSHAW: One of those American bits.

COCKLEBURY-SMYTHE: Quite possibly——

WITHENSHAW: These Americans, they get in everywhere.

COCKLEBURY-SMYTHE: Far too many of them about.

MCTEAZLE: Hear, hear!

CHAMBERLAIN: Absolutely!

WITHENSHAW (*to* MADDIE): Would you care to take my appendix
    out and pass it round—I've something of a reputation for
    dry humour, you know. Yes, I once took a train journey
    right across America . . .

    (*He pauses at the sight of* MADDIE *in her slip.* MADDIE *has*

*picked up the sets of appendices and come out from behind her
desk and taken two steps before remembering her state of
undress, she pauses at the same moment, and then decides to
continue. Big Ben starts chiming the three-quarter hour.*
MADDIE *goes round the table placing documents in front of the
first couple of places. Big Ben finishes chiming the three-
quarter hour.)*

. . . but that's another story.

(The door opens to admit MRS. EBURY. *All look at her as she
speaks except* MCTEAZLE *who tries to hand* MADDIE *her skirt
unnoticed.* MADDIE *misses this, as she is intent on passing out
the rest of the appendices.)*

MRS. EBURY: I'm sorry to be late, Malcolm.

WITHENSHAW: Come right in, Deborah—we're just casting our
eye over the media. You're next to me, lass.

*(*MRS. EBURY *hangs up her coat. She also is carrying newspapers
and case. To get round the table she has to pass behind the
blackboard, as does* MADDIE *who is making slightly heavy
weather of sorting out appendices A, B, C, and D for each
member.* MRS. EBURY *and* MADDIE *cross over behind the
blackboard but do not emerge immediately. Meanwhile the*
CHAIRMAN *has opened the leader page of* The Times *and has
started reading aloud.)*

WITHENSHAW: '*Cherchez La Femme Fatale*. It needs no Gibbon
come from the grave to spell out the danger to good
government of a moral vacuum at the centre of power.
Even so, Rome did not fall in a day, and *mutatis mutandis* it
is not yet a case of *sauve qui peut* for the government——'
—what is all this?—'Admittedly the silence hangs heavy in
the House, no doubt on the principle of *qui s'excuse s'accuse*,
but we expect the electorate to take in its stride *cum grano
salis* stories that upwards of a hundred M.P.s are *in
flagrante delicto*, still more that the *demi-mondaine* in most
cases is a single and presumably exhausted Dubarry *de nos
jours*——' bloody 'ell.

(To MCTEAZLE *who has picked up the* Guardian.)*

What does yours say?

MADDIE (*only her legs visible behind the blackboard*): Forget the

Golden Carriage, the Cooking Pot and the Coq d'Or.
Forget the Golden Carriage, the Watched Pot and the Coq
d'Or. Forget the Golden Pot, Claridges and the Watched
Cook . . .

(MADDIE's *speech is loud until* MCTEAZLE *interrupts with the*
Guardian, *but continues softly until* MCTEAZLE *reaches 'tedious,
or at any rate tendentious . . .' where it stops, to be heard
again on* MCTEAZLE's 'Quis custodiet . . .' *and finally stopping
on* WITHENSHAW's '*Information*'.)

MCTEAZLE (*reading from the* Guardian): '*Spécialités de la Maison.*
The House of Commons is no stranger to scandal or to
farce but it usually manages to arrange its follies so as to
keep the two separate. It would be tedious, or at any rate
tendentious, to give a *catalogue raisonné* of the, at a
Conservative estimate 63 Members of Parliament, and at a
Labour estimate 114, of whom the *homme moyen sensuel* on
the Clapham omnibus might well be asking, "*Quis custodiet
ipsos custodes?*" '

(MRS. EBURY *emerges during this final Latin phrase. Her hair,
which had been done up in a bun, is now about her shoulders
and her buttoned-up suit is in discreet disarray. She takes her
seat.*)

(*Continuing.*) '—and yet our information——'

(MADDIE *emerges from behind the blackboard.*)

WITHENSHAW (*scornfully*): Information! What does the editor of
Manchester Guardian know about anything—bloody young
pup—what's his name——

MADDIE (*putting documents in front of him*): Peter.

WITHENSHAW (*to* MRS. EBURY): Ah—I don't think you know Miss
Gotobed.

MRS. EBURY: How do you do?

(CHAMBERLAIN *picks up the* Daily Mirror.)

CHAMBERLAIN: 'How many cocks on the dung heap? We say too
many—see page 2.' (*He turns the page.*)

(MCTEAZLE *is surreptitiously trying to shove* MADDIE's *skirt at
her as she goes by. She doesn't notice, and he grabs at her
slip.*)

Strewth!

(ALL *but* MCTEAZLE *look at him—*ALL *freeze. Simultaneously* MADDIE's *slip has come away in* MCTEAZLE's *hand, leaving her wearing a revealing blouse, knickers, suspender belt, stockings and shoes.*

After the freeze MADDIE *sits down behind her desk.*

MCTEAZLE *now sits on the skirt and the slip.*)

(*To* MADDIE): Well, are you ready for it Miss Gotobed?

MADDIE: Yes.

WITHENSHAW: Well we seem to be a full complement except for Mr. French. Has anybody heard whether he's coming?

MRS. EBURY: I hope to God not.

WITHENSHAW: Mr. French always has the best interests of the House at heart. That is why he comes over as a sanctimonious busybody with an Energen roll where his balls ought to be—no need to start writing yet, Miss Gotobed.

MCTEAZLE: I don't know what the P.M. was thinking of.

COCKLEBURY-SMYTHE: I expect he was thinking of having a balanced committee to lend the kind of credibility to our report which has eluded him in public life.

WITHENSHAW (*to* MADDIE): Not yet. (*Stands.*) Now, as this Select Committee has, as it were, lost its Chairman of the last session, our first duty as a Committee is to make good that loss.

(*Very rapidly now.*)

COCKLEBURY-SMYTHE: Propose Mr. Withenshaw.

MCTEAZLE: Second.

WITHENSHAW: Any other nominations?

The question is put——

ALL: Aye.

WITHENSHAW: Thank you Mrs. Ebury and gentlemen. (*Sits.*) Let's get started. (*To* MADDIE.) Mr. Withenshaw called to chair. The Chairman's draft report, having been read for the first time—any objections to that?—thank you—was further considered as follows:

Paragraph 1. In performing the duty entrusted to them your Committee took as their guiding principle that it is the just and proper expectation of the electorate and the country at large, that its representatives in Parliament should bring

probity, honourable intent and decent conduct, not merely
to the discharge of the business of government but also to
their personal and social behaviour, which needs must stand
in an exemplary relationship to the behaviour of the British
people generally.

COCKLEBURY-SMYTHE: I must say that strikes an authentic
Lancastrian note. Who wrote this?

WITHENSHAW: Would you mind?

COCKLEBURY-SMYTHE: Was it the P.M.?

WITHENSHAW: No.

COCKLEBURY-SMYTHE: I'll know if it becomes Tennysonian, you
know.

WITHENSHAW: You're out of order, Mr. Cocklebury-Smythe.
(MADDIE *has her hand up, the other hand writing busily but
laboriously.*)
Not that bit, Miss Gotobed.

MADDIE: '. . . called to chair.'

COCKLEBURY-SMYTHE: *The* chair.

WITHENSHAW (*at* MADDIE'*s speed which is about 30 words a
minute*): '*The* chair. The Chair-man's draft report having
been read for the first time was further con-sider-ed as
fol-lows——' The next bit is the draft report which you've
got so you don't have to write it down again.

MADDIE (*with the document*): All this about setting an example?

WITHENSHAW: Yes.

MADDIE: You should tell them to mind their own business.

WITHENSHAW: Who?

MADDIE: Whoever it is who wants to know. It's a load of rubbish.

WITHENSHAW: What is?

MADDIE: People don't care what M.P.s do in their spare time,
they just want them to do their jobs properly bringing
down prices and everything.

WITHENSHAW: Yes, well . . .

MADDIE: Why don't they have a Select Committee to report on
what M.P.s have been up to in their *working* hours—that's
what people want to know.

COCKLEBURY-SMYTHE: It's rather more complicated than that—
er—Arab oil and . . .

(The following speeches overlap each other until the CHAIRMAN *calls the meeting to order.)*

CHAMBERLAIN: . . . the Unions.

COCKLEBURY-SMYTHE: M.P.s don't have the power they used to have, you know.

MCTEAZLE: Foreign exchange—the Bank of England.

MRS. EBURY: The multi-national companies.

MCTEAZLE: Not to mention government by Cabinet.

CHAMBERLAIN: Government by Cabal.

MRS. EBURY: Brussels.

COCKLEBURY-SMYTHE: The Whips.

WITHENSHAW: Just a minute—that'll do—come to order.

MADDIE: I'm sorry.

WITHENSHAW: Paragraph 2. Your Committee took it as self-evident that the consent to govern may be withheld if the people lose respect for the Commons either severally or as an institution, either through executive or constitutional deficiency, either on practical or moral grounds. It is on this latter ground—the morality of the honourable 600—that your Committee has fixed its lance, determined to ride fearlessly into the jaws of controversy.

COCKLEBURY-SMYTHE: It is the P.M., isn't it?

WITHENSHAW: I'm not saying it is, and anyway what's wrong with Her Majesty's first minister keeping a close watch on the interests of the people re clean living on the back benches.

MADDIE: It isn't the people, it's the newspapers.

MCTEAZLE: That's true.

COCKLEBURY-SMYTHE: Well the newspapers *are* the people in a sense—they are the channel of the government's answerability to the governed. The Fourth Estate of the realm speaking for the hearts and minds of the people.

MRS. EBURY: And on top of that they're as smug a collection of inaccurate, hypocritical, self-important, bullying, shoddily printed sick-bags as you'd hope to find in a month of Sundays, and dailies, and the weeklies aren't much better.

COCKLEBURY-SMYTHE: They're not all that inaccurate.

CHAMBERLAIN: You can't ignore them.

MADDIE: Nothing would happen if you did. They've got more people writing about football than writing about you and that's in the *cricket* season—they know what they're about.

COCKLEBURY-SMYTHE: The press, you see, is not just an ordinary commercial enterprise like selling haberdashery.

MADDIE: Yes it is.

COCKLEBURY-SMYTHE: Yes I know it is, but it is also the watchdog of democracy, which haberdashery, by and large, is not.

MADDIE: If the press is all that, you should be asking *them* about chasing after anything in a skirt, which they do. You should have a Select Committee on it—'Your Committee doesn't think it right for journalists to carry on as if there was no tomorrow.'

WITHENSHAW: Thank you——

MADDIE: You're just as entitled to enjoy yourself as they are.

WITHENSHAW: Thank you very much——

MADDIE: You should tell them to mind their own business.

WITHENSHAW: Paragraphs 1 and 2 read and agreed to.

MADDIE: *I* would——

(*The* CHAIRMAN *looks at her.*)

Sorry. (*She starts writing.*)

WITHENSHAW: Paragraph 3.

MADDIE (*with her hand up*): Paragraphs 1 and 2 . . .

WITHENSHAW: . . . read and agreed to. Paragraph 3.

MADDIE (*with her hand up*): . . . read and . . .

WITHENSHAW: . . . agreed to . . .

MADDIE: . . . agreed to . . .

WITHENSHAW: Paragraph 3.

MADDIE: Thank you. Sorry.

WITHENSHAW (*clears throat*): Your Committee and their predecessors in the last session have had before them the papers laid before the House including the written depositions (appendix A) and memoranda (appendix B).

(ALL *turn over to next page.*)

Paragraph 4. Your Committee also had before them a large assortment of press cuttings on this and related matters (appendix C). Your Committee did not feel that any purpose

would be served by calling all the authors of these articles,
which were in any case frequently anonymous or
pseudonymous, and invariably uncorroborated.

MRS. EBURY: Amendment, Mr. Chairman.

WITHENSHAW: Yes, Mrs. Ebury.

MRS. EBURY: Paragraph 4, line 4. After 'invariably uncorroborated' insert 'and actuated by malice'.

WITHENSHAW: Amendment proposed. After 'invariably uncorroborated' insert 'and actuated by malice'. In favour?

ALL (*except* COCKLEBURY-SMYTHE): Aye.

WITHENSHAW: Against.

COCKLEBURY-SMYTHE: No.

WITHENSHAW: Amendment stands. (*To* MADDIE.) All right?

MADDIE: Act . . .

MCTEAZLE: . . . u . . . a . . . (*pause*) . . . ted

CHAMBERLAIN: by . . .

MADDIE: by . . .

COCKLEBURY-SMYTHE: Malice.

MADDIE: Mal . . .

MRS. EBURY: iss . . . (MADDIE *looks up*) . . . *ice*.

WITHENSHAW: Mrs. Ebury in brackets.

MADDIE (*pause*): In brack-ets.

WITHENSHAW: No, no just put her in brackets. (*Apologetically*.)
It's her first time you know.

ALL: Oh yes . . . naturally . . . time to settle down . . .

WITHENSHAW: Very good. Paragraph now ends 'invariably
uncorroborated and actuated by malice'.

CHAMBERLAIN: Amendment, Mr. Chairman.

WITHENSHAW: Yes, Mr. Chamberlain.

CHAMBERLAIN: Insert after 'malice' the words 'and cynical
pursuit of cheap sensationalism'.

WITHENSHAW: Amendment put. In favour?

ALL (*except* COCKLEBURY-SMYTHE): Aye.

WITHENSHAW: Against?

COCKLEBURY-SMYTHE: No.

WITHENSHAW: Amendment stands.

CHAMBERLAIN (*to* MADDIE): Me in brackets.

MADDIE: . . . cyn . . .

CHAMBERLAIN (*at* MADDIE'*s speed*): . . . ical pursuit

MADDIE: . . . ical purs . . .

CHAMBERLAIN: . . . uit of . . .

MADDIE: . . . suit of . . .

CHAMBERLAIN: . . . cheap sens . . .

MADDIE: . . . cheap sense . . .

CHAMBERLAIN: . . . ationalism.

> (*This may have been fractionally faster than the last amendment.*)

MADDIE: . . . ationalism.

WITHENSHAW: That's it. You see you're improving all the time.

ALL: Oh yes . . . getting the hang of it . . .

MCTEAZLE: Amendment, Mr. Chairman. (*He scribbles on a piece of paper.*)

WITHENSHAW: Yes, Mr. McTeazle.

MCTEAZLE: After 'sensationalism' insert 'through a degrading obsession with dirty linen among the Pecksniffs of Fleet Street'. (*He hands paper to* MADDIE.)

WITHENSHAW: I don't think these unnatural practices are very . . .

MCTEAZLE: He's a character in *Dombey and Son*——

WITHENSHAW (*lying*): I am well aware he's a character in *Dombey and Son*.

COCKLEBURY-SMYTHE: Chuzzlewit.

WITHENSHAW (*with spirit*): Chuzzlewit yourself, Cockie. Amendment put. Favour?

ALL (*except* COCKLEBURY-SMYTHE): Aye.

WITHENSHAW: Against.

COCKLEBURY-SMYTHE: No.

WITHENSHAW: Amendment stands. Paragraph now reads——

COCKLEBURY-SMYTHE: Amendment, Mr. Chairman.

WITHENSHAW: Yes, Mr. Cocklebury-Smythe.

COCKLEBURY-SMYTHE: Before the words 'and a cynical pursuit etcetera' insert the words 'in some cases, possibly'.

WITHENSHAW: Amendment put. All in favour?

COCKLEBURY-SMYTHE: Aye.

WITHENSHAW: Against?

ALL (*except* COCKLEBURY-SMYTHE): No.

WITHENSHAW: Amendment fails. (*To* MADDIE.) Paragraph now
    reads . . .

MADDIE (*reading from the draft*): 'Paragraph 4. Your Committee
    also had before them a large assortment of press cuttings on
    this and related matters (appendix C). Your Committee did
    not feel that any purpose would be served by calling all the
    authors of these articles, which were in any case frequently
    anonymous or pseudonymous, and invariably uncorro-
    borated (*reads from her notebook*) and actuated by malice
    and a cynical pursuit of cheap sensationalism (*reads from
    paper passed to her by* MCTEAZLE) through a degrading
    obsession with dirty linen among the Pecksniffs of Fleet
    Street. I'm sitting on your slip. (*To* MCTEAZLE.) Sorry.

MCTEAZLE (*looking at the others*): A slip—just a slip.

WITHENSHAW: The question is put that the paragraph stand as
    part of the report.

COCKLEBURY-SMYTHE: Division, Mr. Chairman.

WITHENSHAW: Division, Committee divided.
    Mr. Chamberlain.

CHAMBERLAIN: Aye.

    (MADDIE'*s hand has gone up.*)

WITHENSHAW (*to* MADDIE): The Com-mit-tee div-id-ed.

MADDIE: . . . divided. Then what do I do?

WITHENSHAW: Then you draw a line down the middle. (*The
    CHAIRMAN goes to the blackboard and draws a line down the
    middle and generally demonstrates on the blackboard. But he
    spells 'noes' as 'Nose'.*) You write 'ayes' up there on the left
    and 'noes' up there on the other side and when I call out
    their names you write them down on one side or the other,
    according to what they say.
    Mr. Chamberlain.

CHAMBERLAIN: Aye.

WITHENSHAW: Mrs. Ebury.

MRS. EBURY: Aye.

WITHENSHAW: Mr. McTeazle.

MCTEAZLE: Aye.

WITHENSHAW: Mr. Cocklebury-Smythe—National Union of
    Journalists.

COCKLEBURY-SMYTHE: No—I have to make a living in my spare time too, you know.

WITHENSHAW: Three—one.

MADDIE: Just like the football results.

WITHENSHAW (*warmly*): Just like the football results. Isn't it?

ALL: Oh yes . . . so it is . . . what a good thought. . . .

WITHENSHAW: Paragraph 4, read and agreed to. Mr. Cocklebury-Smythe, M.P., N.U.J.; dissenting.

Paragraph 5.

MADDIE: You don't need all these paragraphs, you know . . .

WITHENSHAW: 'Your Committee . . .'

MADDIE: You're just playing into their hands.

(WITHENSHAW *glares at her*.)

It's just my opinion.

WITHENSHAW: Paragraph 5. 'Your Committee . . .'

MCTEAZLE (*to* MADDIE): Whose hands?

WITHENSHAW (*to* MCTEAZLE): For God's sake——

MADDIE: The press. The more you accuse them of malice and inaccuracy, the more you're admitting that they've got a right to poke their noses into your private life. All this fuss! The whole report can go straight in the waste-paper basket. All you need is one paragraph saying that M.P.s have got just as much right to enjoy themselves in their own way as anyone else, and Fleet Street can take a running jump.

WITHENSHAW: Miss Gotobed, you may not be aware that the clerk traditionally refrains from drafting the report of a Select Committee.

MADDIE: And anyway, there's no malice in it. You've got that wrong, too.

WITHENSHAW: Paragraph 5!

COCKLEBURY-SMYTHE: She's quite right, of course. It's simplistic to speak of malice.

WITHENSHAW: Smart alec-paragraphs about innocent tripe-and-onions with titian voluptuaries?—if that's not malice I don't know what is.

MADDIE: They only write it up because of each other writing it up. Then they try to write it up *more* than each other—it's like a competition, you see.

COCKLEBURY-SMYTHE (*puzzled*): A free press is competitive
    naturally . . .

MADDIE: No, the *writers*. They're not writing it for the people,
    they're writing it for the writers writing it on the other
    papers. 'Look what I've got that you haven't got.' There
    don't have to be any *people* reading it at all so long as there's
    a few journalists around to say, 'Old Bill got a good one
    there!' That's what they're doing it for. I thought you'd
    have worked that out by now.

COCKLEBURY-SMYTHE (*taken aback*): Not really.

MADDIE: You see, you don't know the first thing about
    journalism.
    (ALL *laugh at* COCKLEBURY-SMYTHE. MADDIE *stands up—*
    unfolds one of the newspapers on her desk and holds it in front
    of her, between her and the Committee so that it obscures her
    skirtless, slipless state of undress from the Committee but not
    from the audience. She walks to the front of the committee
    table. The Committee react to the photograph on the paper
    facing them.)
    The *pictures* are for the people.

ALL: Strewth!
    (*The door opens to admit* MR. FRENCH, *who enters and hangs*
    up his coat. As the Committee look at him, MADDIE *turns and*
    returns to her desk, folding the newspaper.)

CHAMBERLAIN: Hello, French.

FRENCH (*to* CHAIRMAN, *without seeing* MADDIE): Mea maxima
    culpa.

COCKLEBURY-SMYTHE: Merde.

WITHENSHAW: All present and correct. (*To* MADDIE.) Amend list
    of members present.

COCKLEBURY-SMYTHE (*to* MADDIE): French . . .

MADDIE (*to* FRENCH): Enchantée . . .

COCKLEBURY-SMYTHE: No . . . no . . . Mr. French, Miss Gotobed.

FRENCH: How do you do, so sorry to interrupt. (*Looking at the*
    blackboard.) What's that? (*He sits down. He has a white silk*
    handkerchief showing in his breast pocket and he uses this to
    wipe his brow. He does this once or twice during the scene.)

WITHENSHAW: A blackboard. No . . . No . . . I was just . . .

(*He looks round for something to wipe the board but there's nothing to hand so he takes the underpants out of the brief case and uses them.*) . . . our clerk, Miss Gotobed, has been assigned to this Committee on the recommendation of I think you-know-who——

FRENCH: Who?

MADDIE: Fanshawe.

WITHENSHAW: —need I say more? Her experience of committee work is not extensive and I was just explaining one or two of the finer points.

FRENCH: Of course.

WITHENSHAW: Well, as I was saying on that last Division Cocklebury-Smythe is under the 'noes'.

MCTEAZLE: Pecksniff. Chuzzlewit.

COCKLEBURY-SMYTHE: Yes——

MCTEAZLE: Sorry.

COCKLEBURY-SMYTHE: Not at all.

(*The* CHAIRMAN *has hurriedly wiped the board clean and is putting his underpants back into his brief case.*)

FRENCH: What is *that*?

WITHENSHAW: Pair of briefs.

FRENCH: What are they doing in there?

WITHENSHAW: It's a brief case. Paragraph 5.

FRENCH: What stage are we at, Mr. Chairman?

WITHENSHAW: Second reading of the draft report, Mr. French.

FRENCH: When was the first reading?

WITHENSHAW: Haven't you gone through it?

FRENCH: Yes. Last night.

WITHENSHAW: That's when it was. Do you really want me to go through the whole thing again? It's pure formality.

FRENCH: That may be so, but there is a way of doing things, and if we're not going to do them in that way let it be shown in the proceedings of this Select Committee that the Committee voted on that point.

WITHENSHAW: Very well.

(*Very rapidly.*)

COCKLEBURY-SMYTHE: Propose.

MCTEAZLE: Second.

WITHENSHAW: Favour.

ALL (*except* FRENCH): Aye.

WITHENSHAW: Against.

FRENCH: No.

WITHENSHAW: Carried.

> (*Even more rapidly, absolute breakneck speed because it's pure ritual.*)

FRENCH: Division.

WITHENSHAW: Division. Mr. Chamberlain.

CHAMBERLAIN: Aye.

WITHENSHAW: Mr. Cocklebury-Smythe.

COCKLEBURY-SMYTHE: Aye.

WITHENSHAW: Mrs. Ebury.

MRS. EBURY: Aye.

WITHENSHAW: Mr. French.

FRENCH: No.

WITHENSHAW: Mr. McTeazle.

MCTEAZLE: Aye.

WITHENSHAW: Carried.

MADDIE: Line down the middle?

WITHENSHAW: Line down the middle.

> (FRENCH *is slightly surprised by this.*)
>
> Committee divided 4–1.

MADDIE: Home win.

WITHENSHAW: Home win. Mr. French lone scorer for visitors.

FRENCH: I beg your pardon?

WITHENSHAW: The terminology of committee practice is in a constant state of organic change, Mr. French. If you can't keep up you'll be no use to us. Paragraph 5.

FRENCH: Excuse me, Mr. Chairman.

WITHENSHAW: Yes, Mr. French?

FRENCH: We haven't heard any evidence.

WITHENSHAW: Evidence about what, Mr. French?

FRENCH: You know very well, evidence about what—evidence about 128 Members of Parliament making fools of themselves over a latter day Dubarry and bringing the House into public ridicule and disrepute.

WITHENSHAW (*heatedly*): Do you believe everything you read in the papers, Mr. French?

FRENCH (*also heatedly*): I wish to have this exchange of views recorded in the minutes.

WITHENSHAW (*at* MADDIE'*s speed, to* FRENCH): Do you believe everything you read in the papers, Mr. French?

COCKLEBURY-SMYTHE (*at* MADDIE'*s speed, to* FRENCH): It is true that some of us have been feeling up . . .

(*Pause.* ALL *react to 'feeling up' with some trepidation.* COCKLEBURY-SMYTHE *continues innocently.*)

. . . to now that evidence as such does not exist in these matters.

ALL: Hear (*pause*) hear!

(FRENCH *has taken some time to cotton on to the reason for the rate of speech, because the other Members have tactfully ignored* MADDIE. FRENCH *goes through various stages of bewilderment and suspicion before noting* MADDIE'*s writing speed.*)

FRENCH: Just a minute—excuse me—is Miss Gotobed a secretary/clerk of the Clerks Department?

WITHENSHAW: Why d'you ask?

COCKLEBURY-SMYTHE: She can do forty words a minute.

FRENCH: Shorthand?

COCKLEBURY-SMYTHE: No—talking.

MRS. EBURY: She is seconded from the Home Office.

FRENCH: What is her job there? A manicurist?

MADDIE: I'm a typist.

WITHENSHAW: Miss Gotobed has been recommended, by different people, I understand, in a period of some difficulty.

FRENCH: I was expecting to have Mr. Barraclough, a man of irreproachable credentials——

WITHENSHAW: I believe he has taken early retirement for personal reasons.

MADDIE: Barry has?

WITHENSHAW: I must insist that we get on with the proper business of this Committee.

(FRENCH *getting hysterical.*)

FRENCH: The proper business of this Committee is to examine witnesses!

WITHENSHAW: If you will be so patient, Mr. French, you will be reminded that paragraph 5 will take cognizance of the evidence heard by this Select Committee in its previous incarnation during last session.

FRENCH: I was not a member then.

WITHENSHAW: None of us were members then, Mr. French. This Committee has suffered the resignation for personal reasons of the previous membership—and for medical reasons, of the previous chairman, Sir Joshua Matlock who dislocated his hip——

MADDIE: Both hips——

WITHENSHAW: Both hips. Nevertheless that evidence, such as it was, is something which I have given due consideration in preparing this draft report. (*To* MADDIE.) Now. (*Generally, at* MADDIE'*s speed.*) Paragraph 5 read as follows. (*Normal speed.*)
(ALL *turn to proper place in draft report.*)
Your Committee also had the advantage of having a number of distinguished journalists regaling the Committee with the moving and heroic tale of the struggle of the British press from time immemorial to become independent watchdogs of the people's right to know; with many reference to flames, torches, swords, pens, grails and the general impedimenta of chivalrous quest . . .

COCKLEBURY-SMYTHE (*giggles*): Tennyson's Disease.

WITHENSHAW: . . . Unfortunately, the witnesses were con-siderably less helpful on the subject of their sources for the unsubstantiated speculations which were the chief and only reason for the witnesses being called. In the words of Alfred Lord . . . (*pause*) your Committee therefore was unable to conclude that the aforesaid speculations had any basis in fact——

MCTEAZLE: Amendment, Mr. Chairman.

WITHENSHAW: Yes, Mr. McTeazle.

MCTEAZLE: Paragraph 5 line 1 before the word 'journalists' to omit the word 'distinguished'.

FRENCH: Then we should examine the editors.

WITHENSHAW: Can we dispose of this amendment?

FRENCH: What about the leading article in this week's *New Statesman*? It refers to private information.

WITHENSHAW (*jeers*): Private information? Gossiping over Bristol Cream in Vincent Square?

FRENCH: That is your assumption only.

WITHENSHAW: Where else would he pick anything up—young pup—what's-his-name——

MADDIE: Tony.

FRENCH: The editors must be in possession of hard information otherwise they would not let the reporters publish the rumours.

WITHENSHAW: Don't be a fool, man.

COCKLEBURY-SMYTHE: I'm afraid that that does not always follow, Mr. French.

FRENCH: What about *The Times*? You're not suggesting that the editor of *The Times*—a man of irreproachable credentials—— (*Heatedly to* MADDIE.) Mr. French proposed: that the editor of *The Times* . . .

WITHENSHAW: Not so quickly please.

FRENCH (*slowly*): Mr. French proposed . . .

MCTEAZLE (*to* MRS. EBURY): What do you think of it so far?

MRS. EBURY: Rubbish!

FRENCH (*continues slowly*): . . . that the editor of *The Times* (*resuming his normal speed*)—whatever his name is——

MADDIE: Willy.

WITHENSHAW (*impatiently*): This is already dealt with in appendix B. *The Times* has published no rumours, it's only reported facts, namely that less responsible papers are publishing certain rumours. *That* is a written deposition from the editor (*rifling through appendix B*).

FRENCH: It is not. It is a memorandum from one of the Whips who bumped into him in the interval at Covent Garden. Can any one of us truthfully say that we have *really* examined the editor of *The Times*?

CHAMBERLAIN: No.

COCKLEBURY-SMYTHE: No.

WITHENSHAW: No.

MRS. EBURY: No.

MCTEAZLE: No.

MADDIE: Not really.

(Or from Stage Right round the table.)

WITHENSHAW: I must insist that we get back to bloody amendment. The question is put—to omit in line one of paragraph 5 the word 'distinguished' before the word 'journalists'. All in favour.

ALL (*except* COCKLEBURY-SMYTHE *and* FRENCH): Aye.

WITHENSHAW: Against.

COCKLEBURY-SMYTHE: ⎫
FRENCH: ⎬ No.

WITHENSHAW: Arsenal 3 Newcastle 2. Scorers McTeazle, Chamberlain and Ebury for Arsenal. French and Cocklebury-Smythe, own goal, for Newcastle.

FRENCH: What the hell are you talking about?

WITHENSHAW: Kindly watch your language—you're not on terraces now, y'know.

MRS. EBURY: And there are ladies present.

FRENCH: All right! Cards on the table! I didn't want to be the one to bring this up, but I rather expected to learn on arriving here today that one of our number—I exclude Mrs. Ebury of course—had seen fit to resign from this Committee. I refer to the paragraph in today's *Mail* about the tête-à-tête at the Côte d'Or.

MRS. EBURY: Cock.

FRENCH: Coq d'Or.

MRS. EBURY: Double cock.

FRENCH: Without either a resignation or alternatively our joint repudiation of the story I don't see how this Committee can have the confidence of the House.

MRS. EBURY: Ballocks.

FRENCH: That is not an expression which I would have associated with you, Mrs. Ebury.

MRS. EBURY: I don't need you to tell me my problems.

WITHENSHAW (*aside to* MADDIE): The Committee deliberated.

FRENCH: I find the Committee's silence on this point significant.

WITHENSHAW: Well, we all thought it was you.

FRENCH: I left for my constituency on Friday evening and

returned this morning. The only meal I've had this weekend in a London restaurant was tea on Friday at the Golden Egg in Victoria Street.

COCKLEBURY-SMYTHE: L'Oeuf d'Or?

MCTEAZLE: Were you with a woman?

FRENCH: I was with the Dean of St. Paul's.

MCTEAZLE: Is she titian-haired?

CHAMBERLAIN: Come off it McTeazle. (*Kindly to* FRENCH.) French, can anyone corroborate your story?

FRENCH: The Dean of St. Paul's can.

CHAMBERLAIN: Apart from her.

FRENCH: We had Jumbo Chickenburgers Maryland with pickled eggs and a banana milkshake. The waitress will remember me.

CHAMBERLAIN: Why?

FRENCH: I was sick on her shoes.

COCKLEBURY-SMYTHE: Your story smacks of desperation. Even so you have done us the honour of volunteering your account, so let me reciprocate. I was at various times at Crockford's, Claridges and the Golden Cock, Clock, the Old Clock in Golden Square, not the Coq d'Or.

CHAMBERLAIN: I was at the Crock of Gold, Selfridges and the Green Cockatoo.

MCTEAZLE: I was at the Cockatoo, too, and the Charing Cross, the Open Door, the Golden Ox and the Cuckoo Clock.

WITHENSHAW: I was at the Cross Cook, the Fighting Cocks, the Green Door, the Crooked Grin and the Golden Carriages. (*What is happening is difficult to explain but probably quite easy to recognize: the four of them have instinctively joined in an obscuration, each for his own defence. By the time the* CHAIRMAN *speaks they have all begun to send* FRENCH *up.*)

COCKLEBURY-SMYTHE: I forgot—I was at the Golden Carriages as well as Claridges, and the Odd Sock and the Cocked Hat.

WITHENSHAW: I didn't see you at the Cocked Hat—I went on to the Cox and Box.

MCTEAZLE: I was at the Cox and Box, and the Cooks Door, the Old Chest, the Dorchester, the Chesty Cook and—er—Luigi's.

ALL: Luigi's?

MCTEAZLE: At King's Cross.

CHAMBERLAIN: I was at King's Cross; in the Cross Keys and the Coal Hole, the Golden Goose, the Coloured Coat and the Côte d'Azur.

COCKLEBURY-SMYTHE: I was at the Côte d'Azur——

WITHENSHAW: So was I.

MRS. EBURY: I was at the Coq d'Or.

CHAMBERLAIN (*incautiously*): I was at the Coq d'Or too.
(*Short pause but everybody comes to his rescue.*)

MCTEAZLE: So was I.

COCKLEBURY-SMYTHE: The Coq d'Or, oh yes, I was at the Coq d'Or.

WITHENSHAW: I saw you there—I was there with a voluptuous young woman.

COCKLEBURY-SMYTHE: Good heavens, I hope you didn't see me with mine.

CHAMBERLAIN: Fantastic woman I took there—titian hair, green eyes, dress cut down to here.

MCTEAZLE: We held hands under the table—(*with a crude gesture*) voluptuous, you've no idea.

WITHENSHAW: Don't talk to me about voluptuous—mine was titian like two Botticellis fighting their way out of a hammock.
(*During the above speech* FRENCH *is becoming increasingly agitated, and* MADDIE *increasingly angry. She gets out her copy of the* Sun *and opens it to the centre page spread.*)

COCKLEBURY-SMYTHE: Wonderful figure of a woman——

FRENCH (*shouts*): One of you is telling the truth! Where's the *Mail*!
(MADDIE *gets up and crosses to* FRENCH, *holding the* Sun. MADDIE *slams the* Sun *down on the table in front of* FRENCH, *open at the centre page spread and stands back to await his reaction.*)

WITHENSHAW: That's the *Sun*.
(FRENCH *does an enormous double-take at the pin-up.*)

FRENCH (*shrieks*): Aagh!—it's you!!

MADDIE: Yes.

(FRENCH *grabs* MADDIE *by the back of the blouse as she moves to go back to her desk; buttons pop and fly leaving* FRENCH *holding her blouse and* MADDIE *in her bra.*)

ALL (*looking at* MADDIE): Strewth!

(MADDIE *walks to her seat, taps her pencil on the desk.*)

MADDIE (*reading*): Paragraph 6.

FRENCH: Maddie Takes It Down!

'Madeleine Gotobed, twenty-one, is a model secretary in Whitehall where she says her ambition is to be Permanent Under Secretary. Meanwhile, titian-haired, green-eyed Maddie loves being taken out, but says the men tend to look down on a figure like hers—whenever they get the chance!'—disgusting—'Matching bra and suspender belt, Fenwicks £5.35. French knickers, Janet Reger £8.95.' (*To* MADDIE.) You were in the Coq d'Or!

(*The Division Bell goes off.*)

MADDIE: I was in the Coq d'Or, the Golden Ox, Box Hill, Claridges and Crockford's——

WITHENSHAW: Division bell, Mr. French.

MADDIE: —and the Charing Cross, the Dorchester, the Green Cockatoo, Selfridges and the Salt Beef Bar in Rupert Street with Deborah and Douglas and Cockie and Jock.

(MADDIE *has pointed to these four. Pause*—WITHENSHAW *looks relieved.*)

And with Malcolm in the Metropole——

(*The Committee's next words are just rattled off underneath* MADDIE's *speech which continues without pause.*)

WITHENSHAW: Move to adjourn.

COCKLEBURY-SMYTHE: Second.

WITHENSHAW: All in favour.

ALL (*except* FRENCH): Aye.

WITHENSHAW: Meeting adjourned for ten minutes.

(*The Committee hurriedly shuffle a few pieces of paper together, leaving all the newspapers behind, and arrange themselves to make their exits in a body, ignoring* MADDIE, *who chants on.*)

MADDIE (*continuing until all but* FRENCH *have left*): . . . and in the Mandarin, the Mirabelle and the Star of Asia in the Goldhawk Road. I was with Freddie and Reggie and Algy

and Bongo and Arthur and Cyril and Tom and Ernest and
Bob and the other Bob and Pongo at the Ritz and the Red
Lion, the Lobster Pot and Simpson's in the Strand—I was
at the Poule au Pot and the Coq au Vin and the Côte
d'Azur and Foo Luk Fok and the Grosvenor House and
Luigi's and Lacy's and the Light of India with Johnny and
Jackie and Jerry and Joseph and Jimmy, and in the Berkeley,
Biancis, Blooms and Muldoons with Micky and Michael
and Mike and Michelle—I was in the Connaught with
William and in the Westbury with Corkie and in the
Churchill with Chalky. I was at the Duke of York, the Duke
of Clarence and the Old Duke and the King Charles and
the Three Kings and the Kings Arms and the Army and
Navy Salad Bar with Tony and Derek and Bertie and
Plantagenet and Bingo.

(*During the above speech the Committee all exit through the
wrong door, return and re-exit. The door closes, leaving only
*FRENCH *with* MADDIE.)

(*Yells after them.*) And I wouldn't have bothered if I'd
known it was supposed to be a secret—who needs it?
(*Normal voice.*) I sometimes wonder if it's worthwhile
trying to teach people, don't you Mr. French?

FRENCH: Miss Gotobed, this is going to teach them a lesson
they'll never forget.

MADDIE: I hope so.

FRENCH: I have to go and vote. Please be here in about ten
minutes. (*He approaches her with the blouse still in hand.*)

MADDIE: Excuse me . . . (*She takes the blouse.*) . . . Somebody's
coming.

(*At this moment a loud voice is heard approaching.*)
Could you show me the ladies cloakroom.

(*She grabs the rest of her clothes and her handbag.* FRENCH
*takes her coat from the rack and puts it over her shoulders and
opens the door.* MADDIE *exits,* FRENCH *follows. As soon as the
door closes, the other opens and two men enter—but they are
in another play.*)

NEW-FOUND-LAND
A play in one act

Characters

ARTHUR   A very junior Home Office Official
BERNARD   A very senior Home Office Official

The House of Commons overspill meeting room in the tower of Big Ben, set as for Dirty Linen. *A lot of newspapers and reports are lying around on the main committee table.*

(ARTHUR *appears carrying a file of papers and shouts loudly into the door through which he enters, as though calling to someone at a distance.*)

ARTHUR (*shouts*): Here's an empty one!

> (BERNARD *enters immediately.* ARTHUR *shouts at him at the same volume. Everything* ARTHUR *says has to be shouted, throughout.*)
> It's the only one. The Minister said up here—he'll find us all right.
> (*They approach the table and sit at it.*)

BERNARD: Frightful mess.

> (ARTHUR *shuffling newspapers comes across something.*)

ARTHUR: Strewth!!

> (*An appallingly loud noise as Big Ben strikes four from just over their heads.* ARTHUR *flinches.* BERNARD *looks around vaguely. The last stroke finally dies away.*)

BERNARD: What was that?

ARTHUR: Four o'clock.

> (*Considerable pause.* BERNARD *takes out his wallet and an envelope containing a very old £5 note.*)

BERNARD: I bet you have not seen one of these for a while. . . .
It's a fiver I once won off Lloyd George, you know.

ARTHUR: Yes.

BERNARD: It's a good story. . . .

ARTHUR: Very, very good.

BERNARD: I was a green young man at the time, and he was . . .

whatdoyoucallit . . . ?

ARTHUR: Prime Minister.

BERNARD: Prime Minister. Even so, I knew him quite well, or rather my father did.

ARTHUR: Your father knew Lloyd George, yes.

BERNARD: He'd come to our house in Queen Anne Place. You could hear Big Ben from there. That's what reminded me.

ARTHUR: Yes.

This is the file on that applicant for British citizenship. What do you think? (*He moves to sit next to* BERNARD *so that he can speak loudly into his ear. He has a bulky file, including a photograph, to show* BERNARD.)

BERNARD: What?

ARTHUR: These naturalization papers. We're supposed to be advising the Minister.

(BERNARD *examines the document at considerable length.*)

ARTHUR: I'd like to have your opinion.

(*Finally* BERNARD *raps the document authoritatively.*)

BERNARD: This is an application for British naturalization.

ARTHUR: Yes. Does he look all right to you?

BERNARD: He's got a beard. The Minister won't like that.

ARTHUR (*nods*): No, then.

(ARTHUR *closes the file decisively.*)

BERNARD: He asked me for my views about French, you know.

ARTHUR: French?

BERNARD: Poor French. Out of touch. Do you know what he said to me about French?

ARTHUR: Who—the Minister?

BERNARD: Know what he said?

ARTHUR: What?

BERNARD (*shouts*): Do you know what he said about French? (*Normal voice.*) Called him a booby.

ARTHUR (*gives up*): Really.

(*Considerable pause.*)

BERNARD: I was in Belgium, having a look round the village church of Etienne St.-Juste, when I had the good fortune to receive a slight injury. The morning after my return to London, I remember, was one of those rare February days when winter seems to make an envious and premature clutch at the spring to come. I breakfasted by the window. The panes of glass in the window suddenly pulsed (*makes the sound*)—woomph-woomph—as though alive to the shock-waves of distant guns. I started to sob. But it was only a motor coming up the road. It stopped. The doorbell jangled below stairs, and then there was a knock at the morning room. Lloyd George was shown in. My father had already left for the City, as he liked to put it. He owned an emporium of Persian and oriental carpets in Cheapside, which was indeed in the City, and that is where he had gone. So there I was, a young lieutenant, barely blooded, talking to the Prime Minister of the day, and receiving ribald compliments on the shell splinter lodged in my lower abdomen. The shell itself had made a rather greater impact on the church of Etienne St.-Juste. I explained my father's absence, but Lloyd George was in no hurry to leave. It was then that he made his remark about French. 'What do they say in the field?' he asked me. 'Were they glad to see him go?' I replied tactfully that we all felt every confidence in Field-Marshal Haig. 'Yes,' he said, 'Haig's the man to finish this war. French was a booby.' That is what he said. (*Pause.*) Presently, Big Ben was heard to strike ten o'clock. Lloyd George at once asked me whether it was possible to see Big Ben from the upstairs window. I said that it was not. 'Surely you're wrong,' he said, 'are you absolutely certain?' 'Absolutely certain, Prime Minister.' He replied that he found it difficult to believe and would like to see for himself. I assured him that there was no need. The fact was, my mother was upstairs in bed making out her dinner table: she had the understandable, though to me unwelcome, desire to show me off during my leave. Lloyd George pressed the point, and finally said, 'I will bet you £5 that I can see Big Ben from Marjorie's window.' 'Very well,' I said, and we went upstairs. I explained to my mother that the Prime Minister and I had a bet on. She received us gaily, just as though she were in her drawing room, Lloyd George went to the window and pointed.

'Bernard,' he said, 'I see from Big Ben that it is four minutes past the hour. The £5 which you have lost,' he continued, 'I will spend on vast quantities of flowers for your mother by way of excusing this intrusion. It is small price to pay,' he said, 'for the lesson that you must never pit any of the five Anglo-Saxon senses against the Celtic sixth sense.' 'Prime Minister,' I said, 'I'm afraid Welsh intuition is no match for English cunning. Big Ben is the name of the bell, not the clock.' He paid up at once . . .

. . . and that was a fiver which I can tell you I have never spent. (*He shows the note to* ARTHUR.)
How they laughed. 'Marjorie,' he said, 'that boy of yours does not miss a trick.' I left then, to take a cab to Dr. Slocombe in Pall Mall. When I returned I saw Lloyd George alone for the last time. He was coming down the steps. Nervousness caused me to commit the social solecism of trying to return him his money, 'Keep it,' he said, 'I never spent a better £5.' He got into the back of the motor and waved cheerily and called, 'You will go far in the Army.' Well, he was wrong about that. And he was not entirely right about Haig either. It was the Americans who saved *him*.

ARTHUR: This applicant is American.

(*Pause.*)

BERNARD: An *American* with a beard? Oh dear . . . of course, in those days it was the other way round. It was difficult to get British nationality *without* a beard. A well bearded and moustachioed man stood an excellent chance with the Home Secretary. A man with a moustache but no beard was often given the benefit of the doubt. A man with a beard and *no* moustache, on the other hand, was considered unreliable and probably fraudulent, and usually had to remain American for the rest of his life. Does he have property?

(*From here on* ARTHUR *refers to the file.*)

ARTHUR: He is associated with a stable in Kentish Town.

BERNARD: Epsom Downs?

ARTHUR: No—Kentish Town.

BERNARD: A racing stable?

ARTHUR: It seems to be more of a farm really. . . .
    (*Considerable pause.*)
BERNARD: Did you say he farms in Kentish Town?
ARTHUR: Yes.
BERNARD: Arable or pasture?
ARTHUR: It does seem odd doesn't it?
BERNARD: I imagine that good farming land would be at a
    premium in North London. Is he prosperous?
ARTHUR: He has an income of £10.50 per week.
BERNARD: Hardly a pillar of the community, even with free milk
    and eggs.
ARTHUR: No.
BERNARD: He is either a very poor farmer indeed, or a farmer of
    genius—depending on which part of Kentish Town he
    farms.
ARTHUR: He's not exactly a farmer I don't think . . . he has
    other interests. Publishing. And he runs some sort of bus
    service.
BERNARD: Publishing and buses? And a farm. Bit of a gadfly is
    he?
ARTHUR: Yes. And community work.
BERNARD: They all say that.
ARTHUR: Yes.
BERNARD: Anything else?
ARTHUR: There's a theatrical side to him.
BERNARD: Do you mean he waves his arms around?
ARTHUR: No—no—he writes plays, and puts them on and so on.
    He seems to have some kind of theatre.
BERNARD: Oh dear, yes. A theatrical farmer with buses on the
    side, doing publishing and community work in a beard . . .
    are we supposed to tell the Minister that he's just the sort
    of chap this country needs? Does he say why he wants to be
    British?
ARTHUR: Yes, because he's American.
BERNARD: Well he's got a point there.
    Do you know America at all?
ARTHUR: Do I know America!
BERNARD: Americans are a very modern people, of course. They

are a very open people too. They wear their hearts on their
sleeves. They don't stand on ceremony. They take people as
they are. They make no distinction about a man's back-
ground, his parentage, his education. They say what they
mean and there is a vivid muscularity about the way they
say it. They admire everything about them without reserve
or pretence of scholarship. They are always the first to put
their hands in their pockets. They press you to visit them
in their own home the moment they meet you, and are
irrepressibly goodhumoured, ambitious, and brimming with
self-confidence in any company. Apart from all that I've got
nothing against them.

ARTHUR: My America!—my new-found-land! (*He takes
surprising flight.*) Picture the scene as our great ship, with
the blue riband of the Greyhound of the Deep fluttering
from her mizzen, rounds the tolling bell of the Jersey buoy
and with fifty thousand tons of steel plate smashes through
the waters of Long Island Sound. Ahead of us is the golden
span of the Brooklyn Bay Bridge, and on the starboard
quarter the Statue of Liberty herself. Was it just poetic
fancy which made us seem to see a glow shining from that
torch held a thousand feet above our heads?—and to hear
the words of the monumental goddess come softly across
the water: 'Give me your tired, your poor, your huddled
masses, the wretched refuse of your teeming shore . . .'?
The lower decks are crowded with immigrants from every
ghetto in the Continent of Europe, a multitude of tongues
silenced now in the common language of joyful tears.
(*By now* BERNARD *has fallen asleep.*)
The men wave their straw hats. Shawled women hold up
their babies, the newest Americans of all, destined, some of
them, to become the captains and the kings of industrial
empires, to invent the modern age in ramshackle
workshops, to put a chicken into every pot, an automobile
by every stoop, to organize crime as never before, and to fill
the sky over Hollywood with a thousand stars! Nor is the
promenade deck indifferent to the sight. Many a good hand
is abandoned on the bridge tables, many a diamanté purse

forgotten on the zebra-skin divans, as glasses are raised at
the salon windows. New York! New York! It's a wonderful
town! Already we can see the granite cliffs and towers of
Manhattan, and Staten Island too, ablaze like jewels as a
million windows give back the setting sun, and soon we have
set foot on the New World.

The waterfront is seething with life. Here and there milling
gangs of longshoremen scramble on the ground for the
traditional dockets to work the piers, and occasionally two of
them would give savage battle with their loading hooks. At
the intersection of Wall Street with the Bowery the famous
panhandlers, the wretched refuse of cheap barrooms, huddle
in doorways wrapped in copies of the *Journal*. Behind us a
body plummets to the ground—a famous millionaire, we
later discover, now lying broken and hideously smashed
among the miniscule fragments of his gold watch and the
settling flurry of paper bonds bearing the promises of the
Yonkers Silver Mining and Friendly Society. The air is
alive with bells and sirens.

But now a new sound!—ghostly trumpets and trombones
caught in the swirling eddies of the concrete canyons!—and
a few more steps bring us to Broadway. Every way we turn
excited crowds are thronging the electric marquees. Sailors
on shore-leave are doing buck-and-wing dances in and out
of the traffic, at times upon the very roofs of the yellow
taxis bringing John Q. Public and his girl to see the sights
of Baghdad-on-the-Subway. In threes and fours, sometimes
in lines a hundred wide, the midshipmen strut and swing up
the Great White Way chorusing the latest melodies to the
friendly New Yorkers, to the dour Irish policeman swinging
his night-stick on the corner, to the haughty hand-on-hip
ladies of the night who have seen it all before. But it's
time to tip our hats and turn aside, for the tall columned
shadow of Grand Central Station falls across our path. We
are booked on the Silver Chief.

Begging the pardon of a cheerful Redcap we are directed
with a flashing smile to the Chattanooga train. Night is
falling as we cross the Hudson. Friendships are struck,

hipflasks are passed around, and cigar-smoke collects around the poker schools. A cheerful Redcap with a flashing smile fetches ice. The Silver Chief surges through the night. When we retire behind the curtain of our comfortable berths the roaring blackness outside the windows is complete, save for the occasional pillar of fire belching from the mines and mills of Pennsylvania.

And it is to fire that we awake; woods blazing in tangerine shades of burnt umber and old gold—the Fall has come to New England. The train drives relentlessly on, dividing whiteframe villages from their churches, and children from their hoops. And the woods give way to suburbs, and the suburbs to stockyards and slaughter houses, and the wind is slamming off the Great Lake as we pull round the Loop into Chicago—Chicago!—it's a wonderful town! Tight-lipped men in tight-buttoned overcoats and grey fedoras join the poker games. C-notes and G-notes raise the stakes. Shirt-sleeved newspapermen of the old school throw in their cards in disgust and spit tobacco juice upon the well-shined shoes of anyone reading a New York paper. A cheerful shoeshine boy with a flashing smile catches nickels and dimes as he crouches about his business. (*He crosses his legs, revealing Stars and Stripes socks.*) The air is scented with coffee and ham and eggs.

And the countryside is changing too as we swing south. Blue skies and grass are as one on the azure horizon of Kentucky. Soon thoroughbred stallions race the train on either side. Young girls in gingham dresses wave from whitewood fences. But again untamed nature overcomes the pastures—we climb through mountain ash and hickory into the Tennessee Hills. Tumbledown wooden shacks and rusty jalopies give no hint of life but the eye learns to pick out hillbilly groups sullenly looking up from their liquor jugs and washboards.

We doze and wake in thundery oppressive heat. Thick groves of oak and magnolia darken the windows of the speeding train—and encroach, too, upon the fly-blown shutters of white-porticoed mansions which stand decaying sill-high in jungle grasses that once were lawns. Atlanta is burning. A phlegmatic Redcap serves fried chicken and bottles of cherry soda. The poker players have departed. Big-bellied red-eyed men in white crumpled suits swig from medicine bottles of two-year-old sour mash bourbon. Enormous women in taffeta dresses stir the air with pan-handled fans advertising Dr. Pepper Cordials. The train bursts Alabama-bound into the blinding flatlands where cotton is king and a man and mule dominate a thousand acres of unfenced fields like a heroic sculpture. The sun hangs over them like a threat. Our wheels break into clattering echo as the iron girders of the Mississippi Bridge slash across the windows, sending shock-waves to make the glass pulse woomph-woomph around us. Far below, a boy on a raft looks up wistfully at the mournful howl of the Silver Chief, but that old green river rolls them along toward the bend where chanting Negroes heave on the rudder-poles of barges bringing pig-iron from Memphis and hogsheads from St. Louis—and where the last of the river boats working out of Natchez rides the oily waters like a painted castle way down yonder to New Orleans.

The train slows, crawling through the French quarter of the City on the Delta. The sun hangs like a copper pan over boarding houses with elaborately scrolled gingerbread eaves. In the red-lit shadow of wrought-iron balconies octaroon Loreleis sing their siren songs to shore-leave sailors, and sharp-suited pimps push open saloon doors, spilling light and ragtime to underscore the street cries of old men selling shrimp gumbo down on the levee. A dignified Redcap hums an eight-bar blues—how long, how long, has that evening train been gone?—At the back of the car a one-armed white man takes a battered cornet from inside his shirt and picks up the tune with pure and plangent notes. Soon the whole car—Bible salesmen, buck privates from Fort Dixie, majorettes from L.S.U., farm boys and a couple of nuns—is singing the blues in the night. (*He lights a cigarette— American brand.*) The sun drops into the smoke stacks of Galveston like a dirty dinner plate behind a sofa. The train picks up speed. When we retire behind the curtains of our comfortable berths the roaring blackness outside the windows is complete save for the occasional pillar of fire flaring up from oil wells under the cooling scrub.

BERNARD (*waking up*): Ever seen one of these before, Arthur?—I won this fiver off——

ARTHUR (*violently*): Ten thousand head of cattle on the hoof, packed together in a rolling river of hide and horn, meet our eye when we are woken with steak and eggs by a surly Redcap! The Silver Chief is on the Chisholm trail to Abilene! Amarillo—Laramie—El Paso—Dodge! The wheels roll, the rails curve, past the crude wooden crosses of Boot Hill where other lean-jawed men who once rode tall now lie in gunslingers' graves. (*He reveals a Sheriff's star on his waistcoat.*) And beyond, the open prairie. Tumbleweed races the train on either side. Lone riders whoop and wave their hats from lathering ponies and are lost to sight as we hit the dustbowls of Oklahoma! Where once the corn stood high as an elevator boy, and the barns shook with dancing farmhands changing partners to a fiddler's call, now screen doors bang endlessly in the wind which long ago covered up the tyre tracks of bone-rattling pick-ups taking the Okies on their tragic exodus to the promised lands of El Dorado. How easy now on the gleaming rails, now carving a path through the heart of the grain lands where the gigantic mantis-forms of harvesters trawl the golden ocean that fills the breadbaskets of America!

We climb with the sun out of the plains . . . Carson City—Sioux City—Tucson—Tulsa—Albuquerque—Acheson, Topeka and the Sante Fé—Wichita. . . . Snow-capped mountains shimmer on the horizon, and still we climb. From the observation platform at the rear we watch the shadows turn the thousand-foot walls of the Colorado River deep red and purple. Huddled in our blanket we sleep. Once we seem to wake to a nightmare of acrylic lights—against a magenta sky huge electric horseshoes, dice, roulette wheels and giant Amazons with tasselled breasts change colour atop marble citadels that would beggar Kubla Khan. But when the

cheerful Redcap shakes us all is peace. The Silver Chief is
rolling through vineyards and orchards, a sun-bathed
Canaan decked with peach and apricot, apples, plums,
citrus fruit and pomegranates, which grow to the very walls
of pink and yellow bungalows to the very edge of swimming
pools where near-naked goddesses with honey-brown skins
rub oil into their long downy limbs. Could this be paradise?
—or is it after all, purgatory?—for look!—there, where
picture palaces rise from the plain, searchlights and letters
of fire light up the sky, and a screaming hydra-headed mob
surges, fighting and weeping, around an unseen idol—golden
calf or Cadillac, we do not stop to see—for now beyond the
city, beyond America, beyond all, nothing lies before us but
an endless expanse of blue, flecked with cheerful whitecaps.
With wondering eyes we stare at the Pacific, and all of us
look at each other with a wild surmise—silent——
(*The door opens. Several men and a woman barge in as though
they owned the place, chatting among themselves.*)
I think you got the wrong room, buster.

DIRTY LINEN
concluded

The room is occupied by two men, both Home Office Civil Servants, both formally dressed (ARTHUR and BERNARD).

ARTHUR *has a file of papers among other paraphernalia.*

(*The door opens and in come* WITHENSHAW, COCKLEBURY-SMYTHE, MCTEAZLE, MRS. EBURY *and* CHAMBERLAIN, *chatting.* WITHENSHAW *goes to confront* ARTHUR *at the secretary/clerk's desk.*)

WITHENSHAW: What?

ARTHUR: I'm sorry—this is a Home Office Departmental Meeting.

WITHENSHAW: What are you doing here?

ARTHUR: We are meeting here for the convenience of the Home Secretary who has to answer the Division Bell.

WITHENSHAW: Well, I'm very sorry, but as you can see this room is occupied by a Select Committee.

ARTHUR: On the contrary, as you can see, it is occupied by a Home Office Departmental Meeting.

WITHENSHAW: Yes, but we were here first.

MCTEAZLE: Hello, Bernard—still soldiering on?

BERNARD (*standing up*): Mr. McTeazle, isn't it?—yes—yes—I was just showing young Arthur here—I bet you haven't seen one of these for a while (*produces £5 note*).
(*Meanwhile* WITHENSHAW *is writing another note for* MADDIE. *By this time* COCKLEBURY-SMYTHE, MCTEAZLE, CHAMBERLAIN *and* MRS. EBURY *have sat down. The* HOME SECRETARY *enters with a rush of words and sits in the Chairman's place.*)

HOME SECRETARY: Good afternoon, gentlemen—what a large gathering—difficult case?—I thought it was only that American—goodness me, let's keep things tidy can we?
(*He starts stacking the mess of newspapers on the table.*) An

orderly table makes for an orderly meeting. (*He has the Mirror in his hands.*) Strewth!

Tit-tit-tut-tut-oh! (*Sees* WITHENSHAW *whilst folding the pin-up picture away.*) Hello Malcolm.

ARTHUR: This lady and these gentlemen are here for another meeting, Minister.

WITHENSHAW: Sorry, Reg, first come first served.

HOME SECRETARY: Are you Send-In-A-Gumboot?

WITHENSHAW: What?

HOME SECRETARY: Are you Rubber Goods Import Quota?

WITHENSHAW: No—no—we're Moral Standards in Public Life.

HOME SECRETARY: Oh yes, so you are—no hard information, I hear.

WITHENSHAW: We're not sure, Reg—something came up this afternoon.

HOME SECRETARY: Yes, well, I'm sorry to pull rank on you, Malcolm . . .

(*The Select Committee Members stand up;* ARTHUR *and* BERNARD *sit down.*)

. . . but I've got to deal with a very sensitive and difficult case——

(*The* HOME SECRETARY *picks up* WITHENSHAW'*s note to* MADDIE, *who by this point has entered and is hanging up her coat.*)

What's this? 'Forget Claridges, the Olden Bottle . . .'

(WITHENSHAW *snatches it out of his hand and tears it into four and scatters the pieces.*)

MADDIE (*to* HOME SECRETARY): Hello, what are you doing here?

HOME SECRETARY: How do you do? My name's Jones. (*To* WITHENSHAW.) As I was saying you must have the room of course.

(ARTHUR *and* BERNARD *stand up,* WITHENSHAW *crosses to his Chairman's seat and the Select Committee sit down again. The* HOME SECRETARY *continues, the italicized words aside to* MADDIE.)

Noblesse oblige—say no more—anyway I'm expected at an Intrusion of Privacy Sub-Committee of the *Forget Le Coq au Vin and La Poule au Pot* Departmental Committee on Rag and Bone Men, Debt Collectors and Journalists.

ARTHUR: But Minister what about . . . ?

(ARTHUR *holds out the folder. The* HOME SECRETARY *whips out a pen and signs with a flourish.*)

HOME SECRETARY: One more American can't make any difference.

(BERNARD *approaches* WITHENSHAW *with the £5 note.*)

BERNARD: Mr. Withenshaw, isn't it? Take a look at this—there's quite a story behind it——

(WITHENSHAW *snatches the note and tears it into four pieces.* BERNARD *is crestfallen.*)

WITHENSHAW (*shouts*): Get out!

HOME SECRETARY: A word in your ear, Malcolm. Have you got time for a drink?

(*The Home Office men leave.*)

WITHENSHAW: Well . . .

(FRENCH *enters and crosses to his place.*)

. . . not really Reg.

HOME SECRETARY: I'll give you a ring.

(*The* HOME SECRETARY *leaves. An uncomfortable silence descends as the Select Committee settle down.*)

WITHENSHAW: Well now . . . where were we . . .

(*Pause.*)

FRENCH: Mr. Chairman . . .

WITHENSHAW: Oh yes . . . you were about to make a point, Mr. French.

FRENCH: Thank you Mr. Chairman. I have been giving this matter a great deal of thought during our short adjournment. I think I can say that never has the phrase *O tempora O mores* come so readily to the lips.

COCKLEBURY-SMYTHE: Meaning what?

FRENCH: Meaning, 'Oh the times Oh the——'

COCKLEBURY-SMYTHE: I know what it means. Why was it on your lips?

FRENCH: I am not a whited sepulchre, Mr. Chairman. I take no pleasure in crying 'j'accuse'. But I have been talking to Miss Gotobed. She has poured out her heart to me and I may say it was a *mauvais quart d'heure* for the Mother of Parliaments. Not since Dunkirk have so many people been in the same boat—proportionately speaking. I am faced now

with a responsibility which I would dearly like to be
without, but it seems I am presented with, to put it in plain
English, a *fait accompli*. I have struggled with my
conscience seeking an honourable course and not wishing to
drag this noble institution through the mud.

WITHENSHAW: A very responsible attitude, Mr. French.

MCTEAZLE: ⎫
　　　　　 ⎬ Hear, hear!
CHAMBERLAIN: ⎭

FRENCH: Thank you. I think I have indeed found a way. I
propose we scrap the Chairman's Report as it stands and
replace it with a new report of my own drafting. (*He holds
up a piece of paper. He clears his throat and starts to read.*)
Paragraph 1. In performing the duty entrusted to them
your Committee took as their guiding principle that it is the
just and proper expectation of every Member of Parliament,
no less than for every citizen of this country, that what they
choose to do in their own time, and with whom, is . . .

MADDIE (*prompting*): . . . between them and their conscience.

FRENCH (*simultaneously with* MADDIE): . . . conscience, provided
they do not transgress the rights of others or the law of the
land; and that this principle is not to be sacrificed to that
Fleet Street stalking-horse masquerading as a sacred cow
labelled 'The People's Right to Know'.

　　　Your Committee found no evidence or even suggestion of
laws broken or harm done, and thereby concludes that its
business is hereby completed.

WITHENSHAW: Is that it?

FRENCH: It's the best I can do.

WITHENSHAW: How am I going to spin that out until Queen's
Jubilee?

FRENCH: You can't. This is the last meeting of this Committee,
unless you want to do it your way.

WITHENSHAW: No—no——

　　　(MADDIE *throws her report and all her appendices in the
waste-paper basket.*)

COCKLEBURY-SMYTHE: You'll have to get your peerage another
way.

WITHENSHAW: The P.M. will kick my arse from here to Blackpool.

COCKLEBURY-SMYTHE: Services to sport.

MCTEAZLE: I would like to applaud Mr. French's understanding attitude and his stroke of diplomacy.

CHAMBERLAIN: Hear, hear.

MRS. EBURY: I move that Mr. French's report is put to the Committee.

COCKLEBURY-SMYTHE: Second.

WITHENSHAW: Have you got that, Miss Gotobed?

MADDIE: Yes, Malcolm.

WITHENSHAW: All in favour.

ALL: Aye.

WITHENSHAW: Against.

(*Silence.*)

FRENCH: Arsenal 5—Newcastle nil.

WITHENSHAW: Thank you, Mr. French.

FRENCH: Not at all, Mr. Chairman. (*He takes out his breast-pocket handkerchief, which is now the pair of knickers put on by* MADDIE *at the beginning, and wipes his brow.*) Toujours l'amour.

(*Big Ben chimes the quarter hour.*)

MADDIE: Finita La Commedia.

DOGG'S HAMLET,

INTRODUCTION

The comma that divides *Dogg's Hamlet, Cahoot's Macbeth* also
serves to unite two plays which have common elements: the first
is hardly a play at all without the second, which cannot be
performed without the first.

Dogg's Hamlet is a conflation of two pieces written for Ed
Berman and Inter-Action; namely *Dogg's Our Pet*, which opened
the Almost Free Theatre in Soho in December 1971, and *The
Dogg's Troupe 15-Minute Hamlet*, which was written (or rather
edited) for performance on a double-decker bus.

Dogg's Hamlet derives from a section of Wittgenstein's
philosophical investigations. Consider the following scene.
A man is building a platform using pieces of wood of different
shapes and sizes. These are thrown to him by
a second man, one at a time, as they are called for. An
observer notes that each time the first man shouts 'Plank!'
he is thrown a long flat piece. Then he calls 'Slab!' and
is thrown a piece of a different shape. This happens a few times.
There is a call for 'Block!' and a third shape is thrown.
Finally a call for 'Cube!' produces a fourth type of piece. An
observer would probably conclude that the different words
described different shapes and sizes of the material. But this is
not the only possible interpretation. Suppose, for example, the
thrower knows in advance which pieces the builder needs, and in
what order. In such a case there would be no need for the
builder to name the pieces he requires but only to indicate when
he is ready for the next one. So the calls might translate thus:

Plank = Ready   Block = Next
Slab = Okay   Cube = Thank you

In such a case, the observer would have made a false
assumption, but the fact that he on the one hand and the
builders on the other are using two different languages need not

be apparent to either party. Moreover, it would also be possible that the two builders do not share a language either; and if life for them consisted only of building platforms in this manner there would be no reason for them to discover that each was using a language unknown to the other. This happy state of affairs would of course continue only as long as, through sheer co-incidence, each man's utterance made sense (even if not the same sense) to the other.

The appeal to me consisted in the possibility of writing a play which had to teach the audience the language the play was written in. The present text is a modest attempt to do this: I think one might have gone much further.

Cahoot's Macbeth is dedicated to the Czechoslovakian playwright Pavel Kohout. During the last decade of 'normalization' which followed the fall of Dubcek, thousands of Czechoslovaks have been prevented from pursuing their careers. Among them are many writers and actors.

During a short visit to Prague in 1977 I met Kohout and Pavel Landovsky, a well-known actor who had been banned from working for years since falling foul of the authorities. (It was Landovsky who was driving the car on the fateful day in January 1977 when the police stopped him and his friends and seized the first known copies of the document that became known as Charter 77.) One evening Landovsky took me backstage at one of the theatres where he had done some of his best work. A performance was going on at the time and his sense of fierce frustration is difficult to describe.

A year later Kohout wrote to me: 'As you know, many Czech theatre-people are not allowed to work in the theatre during the last years. As one of them who cannot live without theatre I was searching for a possibility to do theatre in spite of circumstances. Now I am glad to tell you that in a few days, after eight weeks rehearsals—a Living-Room Theatre is opening, with nothing smaller but Macbeth.

'What is LRT? A call-group. Everybody, who wants to have Macbeth at home with two great and forbidden Czech actors, Pavel Landovsky and Vlasta Chramostova, can invite his friends and call us. Five people will come with one suitcase.

'Pavel Landovsky and Vlasta Chramostova are starring Macbeth and Lady, a well known and forbidden young singer Vlastimil Tresnak is singing Malcolm and making music, one young girl, who couldn't study the theatre-school, Tereza Kohoutova, by chance my daughter, is playing little parts and reading remarks; and the last man, that's me . . .! is reading and a little bit playing the rest of the roles, on behalf of his great colleague.

'I think, he wouldn't be worried about it, it functions and promises to be not only a solution of our situation but also an interesting theatre event. I adapted the play, of course, but I am sure it is nevertheless Macbeth!'

The letter was written in June, and in August there was a postscript: 'Macbeth is now performed in Prague flats.'

Cahoot's Macbeth was inspired by these events. However, Cahoot is not Kohout, and this necessarily over-truncated *Macbeth* is not supposed to be a fair representation of Kohout's elegant seventy-five minute version.

TOM STOPPARD
August 1980

Dogg's Hamlet is
dedicated to
Professor Dogg
and The Dogg's Troupe
of Inter-Action

CHARACTERS

BAKER
ABEL
CHARLIE
EASY
DOGG
LADY
FOX MAJOR
MRS DOGG
SHAKESPEARE
HAMLET
HORATIO
CLAUDIUS
GERTRUDE
POLONIUS
OPHELIA
LAERTES
GHOST
BERNARDO
FRANCISCO
GRAVEDIGGER
OSRIC
FORTINBRAS

The first stage performance of *Dogg's Hamlet, Cahoot's Macbeth* was at the Arts Centre of the University of Warwick, Coventry, on 21 May 1979, by BARC, British American Repertory Company. The cast of BARC was:

John Challis
Alison Frazer
Ben Gotlieb
Peter Grayer
Davis Hall
Louis Haslar
Ruth Hunt
Stanley McGeagh
Stephen D. Newman
John Straub
Alan Thompson
Sarah Venable
Gilbert Vernon

Designed by Norman Coates
Directed by Ed Berman

The play opened for a season at the Collegiate Theatre, London, on 30 July 1979.

Translation from 'Dogg' language into English is given in square brackets where this seems necessary.

Empty stage.
BAKER: (*Off-stage*) Brick! [*Here!]
    (*A football is thrown from off-stage left to off-stage right.*
    BAKER *receiving ball*) Cube. [*Thanks]
    (ABEL, *off-stage, throws satchel to stage left.* ABEL *enters. He is a schoolboy wearing grey flannel shorts, blazer, school cap, etc., and carrying a satchel. He drops satchel centre stage and collects the other which he places with his own.* ABEL *exits stage right and returns with microphone and stand which he places down stage. The microphone has a switch.*)
ABEL: (*Into the microphone*) Breakfast, breakfast . . . sun—dock—trog . . . [*Testing, testing . . . one—two—three . . .]
    (*He realizes the microphone is dead. He tries the switch a couple of times and then speaks again into the microphone.*)
    Sun—dock—trog—pan—slack . . . [*One—two—three—four—five . . .]
    (*The microphone is still dead.* ABEL *calls to someone off-stage.*)
    Haddock priest! [*The mike is dead!]
    (*Pause.* BAKER *enters from the same direction. He is also a schoolboy similarly dressed.*)
BAKER: Eh? [*Eh?]
ABEL: Haddock priest.
BAKER: Haddock?
ABEL: Priest.
    (BAKER *goes to the microphone, drops satchel centre on his way.*)
BAKER: Sun—dock—trog—
    (*The mike is dead.* BAKER *swears.*) Bicycles!
    (BAKER *goes back off-stage. Pause. The loud-speakers crackle.*)
ABEL: Slab? [*Okay?]
BAKER: (*Shouting off-stage, indistinctly.*) Slab!
ABEL: (*Speaking into the mike.*) Sun, dock, trog, slack, pan.

(*The mike is live.* ABEL *shouting to* BAKER, *with a thumbs-up sign.*)

Slab! [*Okay!]

(*Behind* ABEL, CHARLIE, *another schoolboy, enters backwards, hopping about, the visible half of a ball-throwing game.* CHARLIE *is wearing a dress, but schoolboy's shorts, shoes and socks, and no wig.*)

CHARLIE: Brick! . . . brick! [*Here! . . . here!]

(*A ball is thrown to him from the wings.* ABEL *dispossesses* CHARLIE *of the ball.*)

ABEL: Cube! [*Thanks!]

VOICE: (*Off-stage*) Brick! [*Here!]

(CHARLIE *tries to get the ball but* ABEL *won't let him have it.*)

CHARLIE: Squire! [*Bastard!]

(ABEL *throws the ball to the unseen person in the wings—not where* BAKER *is.*)

Daisy squire! [*Mean bastard!]

ABEL: Afternoons! [*Get stuffed!]

CHARLIE: (*Very aggrieved.*) Vanilla squire! [*Rotten bastard!]

ABEL: (*Giving a V-sign to* CHARLIE.) Afternoons!

(ABEL *hopping about, calls for the ball from the wings.*)

Brick! [*Here!]

(*The ball is thrown to* ABEL *over* CHARLIE'S *head.* DOGG, *the headmaster, in mortar-board and gown, enters from the opposite wing, and as the ball is thrown to* ABEL, DOGG *dispossesses* ABEL.)

DOGG: Cube! [*Thank you!] Pax! [*Lout!]

(DOGG *gives* ABEL *a clip over the ear and starts to march off carrying the ball.*)

ABEL: (*Respectfully to* DOGG.) Cretinous, git? [*What time it is, sir?]

DOGG: (*Turning round.*) Eh?

ABEL: Cretinous pig-faced, git? [*Have you got the time please, sir?]

(DOGG *takes a watch out of his waistcoat pocket and examines it.*)

DOGG: Trog poxy. [*Half-past three.]

ABEL: Cube, git. [*Thank you, sir.]

DOGG: Upside artichoke almost Leamington Spa? [*Have you
  seen the lorry from Leamington Spa?]

ABEL: Artichoke, git? [*Lorry, sir?]

CHARLIE: Leamington Spa, git? [*Leamington Spa, sir?]

DOGG: Upside? [*Have you seen it?]

ABEL: (*Shaking his head.*) Nit, git. [*No, sir.]

CHARLIE: (*Shaking his head.*) Nit, git. [*No, sir.]

DOGG: (*Leaving again.*) Tsk. Tsk. [*Tsk. Tsk.] Useless. [*Good
  day.]

ABEL/CHARLIE: Useless, git. [*Good day, sir.]

  (DOGG *exits with the ball.* BAKER *enters. He looks at his wrist
  watch.*)

BAKER: Trog poxy. [*Half-past three.]

  (*There are now three satchels on the ground centre stage.*
  BAKER *goes to one and extracts a packet of sandwiches.* ABEL
  and CHARLIE *do the same. The three boys settle down and start
  to examine their sandwiches.*)

ABEL: (*Looking in his sandwiches.*) Pelican crash. [*Cream cheese.]
  (*To* BAKER.) Even ran? [*What have you got?]

BAKER: (*Looking in his sandwich.*) Hollyhocks. [*Ham.]

ABEL: (*To* CHARLIE.) Even ran? [*What have you got?]

CHARLIE: (*Looking in his sandwich.*) Mouseholes. [*Egg.]

ABEL: (*To* CHARLIE.) Undertake sun pelican crash frankly sun
  mousehole? [* Swop you one cream cheese for one egg?]

CHARLIE: (*With an amiable shrug.*) Slab. [*Okay.]

  (ABEL *and* CHARLIE *exchange half a sandwich each.*)

BAKER: (*To Abel.*) Undertake sun hollyhocks frankly sun pelican
  crash?

ABEL: Hollyhocks? Nit!

BAKER: Squire!

ABEL: Afternoons!

  (BAKER *fans himself with his cap and makes a comment about
  the heat.*)

BAKER: Afternoons! Phew—cycle racks hardly butter fag ends.
  [*Comment about heat.]

CHARLIE: (*Agreeing with him.*) Fag ends likely butter
  consequential.

ABEL: Very true. [*Needs salt.]

CHARLIE: Eh?

ABEL: (*Putting out his hand.*) Very true.

(CHARLIE *takes a salt cellar out of his satchel.* CHARLIE *passes* ABEL *the salt.*)

Cube. [*Thank you.]

(*He sprinkles salt on his sandwich and then offers salt to* BAKER.) Very true? [*Need salt?]

BAKER: (*Taking it.*) Cube. [*Thank you.]

(BAKER *uses the salt and puts it down next to him.* CHARLIE *puts his hand out towards* BAKER.)

CHARLIE: Brick. [*Here.]

(BAKER *passes* CHARLIE *his salt-cellar. They eat their sandwiches. The explanation for the next passage of dialogue is that* ABEL *and* BAKER, *who are due shortly to participate in a school play performed in its original language—English—start rehearsing some of their lines.*)

ABEL: (*Suddenly*) Who's there?

BAKER: Nay, answer me.

ABEL: Long live the King. Get thee to bed.

BAKER: For this relief, much thanks.

(ABEL *stands up.*)

ABEL: What, has this thing appeared again tonight?

(BAKER *stands up by him.*)

BAKER: Peace, break thee off: look where it comes again.

ABEL: Looks it not like the King?

(*They are not acting these lines at all, merely uttering them, tonelessly.*)

BAKER: By heaven, I charge thee, speak!

ABEL: 'Tis here. (*Pointing stage left.*)

BAKER: 'Tis there. (*Pointing stage right, their arms crossing awkwardly.*)

ABEL: 'Tis gone.

BAKER: But look—the russet mantle . . .

(*He has gone wrong. Pause.*)

ABEL: (*Trying to help him.*) Clad—walks . . .

(ABEL *and* BAKER *don't always structure their sentences correctly.*)

BAKER: (*Shakes his head and swears softly to himself.*)

Bicycles!

(BAKER *produces from his pocket his script. He looks through it and finds where he has gone wrong.*)

> The *morn*!—the morn in russet mantle clad—walks
> o'er the dew of yon high eastern hill.

ABEL: Let us impart what we have seen tonight unto (*indicating* HAMLET *is just above waist height with his hand.*) young Hamlet . . . Slab? [*Okay?] Block. [*Next.]

(BAKER *shakes his head and sits down.*)

BAKER: (*Shakes head.*) Nit! [*No!]

(CHARLIE, *for no reason, is singing to the tune of 'My Way'. He doesn't know all the words in the third line.* BAKER *joins in on the fourth line in close harmony.*)

CHARLIE: (*Sings*) Engage congratulate moreover state abysmal
> fairground.
> Begat perambulate this aerodrome chocolate eclair
> found.
> Maureen again dedum-de-da- ultimately cried egg.
> Dinosaurs rely indoors if satisfied egg . . .

(ABEL *blows a raspberry by way of judgement. As the song dies away a lorry is heard arriving. The three boys get up and put away their sandwich papers etc. and look expectantly in the direction of the lorry.*)

BAKER: Artichoke. [*Lorry.]

(BAKER *goes forward, looking out into the wings, and starts directing the lorry—which is apparently backing towards him— with expressive gestures.*)

Cauliflower . . . cauliflower . . . hardly . . . onyx hardly . . . [*Left . . . left . . . right . . . right hand down . . .] Tissue . . . tissue . . . slab! [*Straight . . . straight . . . okay!]

(*The lorry-driver* EASY *is heard slamming the cab door and he enters. He is dressed in a white boiler-suit and cloth cap and is carrying a rolled-up red carpet and a box of small flags on sticks. He puts them down.*)

EASY: Buxton's—blocks an' that.

ABEL: Eh?

EASY: Buxton's Deliveries of Leamington Spa. I've got a load of blocks and that. I'll need a bit of a hand.

(*Pause. The boys look at him blankly, baffled.*)

ABEL: Eh?

EASY: I'll need a bit of a hand, being as I'm on my own, seeing
as my mate got struck down in a thunderstorm on the A412
near Rickmansworth—a bizarre accident . . . a bolt from the
blue, zig-zagged right on to the perforated snout of his Micky
Mouse gas mask. He was delivering five of them at the
bacteriological research children's party—entering into the
spirit of it—when, shazam!—it was an electrifying moment,
left his nose looking more like Donald Duck and his ears like
they popped out of a toaster. He sounded like a cuckoo clock
striking twelve.

(EASY *relates story with considerable gusto, but to his
disappointment it falls flat being, of course, not understood.*)
Right you are then, lads. Where do you want them?

(*Another long pause.* BAKER *takes a step forward towards* EASY,
pleased with himself for having a good idea.)

BAKER: By heaven I charge thee speak!

(*Pause.*)

EASY: Who are you then?

BAKER: (*Encouragingly.*) William Shakespeare.

EASY: (*To* ABEL.) Cretin is he?

BAKER: (*Looking at his wrist watch.*) Trog-taxi.

EASY: I thought so. (*Looking at* CHARLIE.) Are you all a bit
peculiar, then? Where's the guvnor?

(DOGG *enters briskly.*)

DOGG: Useless! [*Afternoon!]

BOYS: Useless, git! [*Afternoon, sir!]

EASY: Afternoon, squire. [This means in Dogg, *Get stuffed, you
bastard.]

(DOGG *grabs* EASY *by the lapels in a threatening manner.*)

DOGG: Marzipan clocks! [*Watch it!]

(DOGG *produces a piece of paper which is a plan of the
construction which is to be made on the stage. This is quite a
large piece of paper and the steps and wall which are to be built
are discernible on it.* DOGG *examines the paper briefly and then
starts positioning the boys.*)

Abel . . .

ABEL: Slab, git. [*Yes, sir.]

DOGG: (*Pointing towards the lorry.*) Pontoon crumble.

ABEL: Slab, git.

(*ABEL goes out towards the lorry.*)

DOGG: Baker . . .

(*BAKER pays attention.*)

Brick. [*Here.]

(*He positions BAKER next to the wing near the lorry.*)

BAKER: Slab, git.

DOGG: Cube. [*Thank you.] (*To CHARLIE.*) Charlie.

CHARLIE: Slab, git.

DOGG: Brick.

(*He positions CHARLIE in line with BAKER and the lorry. EASY stands next CHARLIE in the place where the steps are to be built. To BAKER and CHARLIE.*) Plank? [*Ready?]

BAKER/CHARLIE: Plank, git. [*Ready, sir.]

DOGG: (*Calling out to ABEL.*) Plank?

ABEL: (*Off-stage.*) Plank, git.

(*DOGG gives the piece of paper to EASY who studies it warily. EASY puts the paper in his pocket.*)

DOGG: (*Calling out to ABEL loudly—shouts.*) Plank!

(*To EASY's surprise and relief a plank is thrown to BAKER who catches it, passes it to CHARLIE, who passes it to EASY, who places it on the stage. DOGG smiles, looks encouragingly at EASY.*)

EASY: (*Uncertainly, calls.*) Plank!

To his surprise and relief a second plank is thrown in and passed to him the same way. He places it.)

Plank!

(*A third plank is thrown in and positioned as before. DOGG leaves, satisfied. Note: EASY is going to build a platform, using 'planks', 'slabs', 'blocks' and 'cubes' so that the platform is stepped, with the steps upstage.*

Confidently, calls.) Plank!

(*A block is thrown instead of a plank. When it reaches EASY, he passes it back to CHARLIE who passes it back to BAKER, who turns and places it on the floor upstage. While BAKER is upstage EASY has repeated his call.*)

Plank!!

(*A second block is thrown straight into* CHARLIE's *arms.*
CHARLIE *passes it to* EASY *who passes it back to* CHARLIE *who
takes it upstage to join the first block on the floor.* EASY *shouts.*)
Plank!!!

(*A plank is thrown straight to him and he places it gratefully
on the floor next to the other three.* EASY *takes another look at
the plans and replaces them into his pocket. He shouts.*)
Slab!

(BAKER *and* CHARLIE *have resumed their positions. A slab is
thrown in, caught by* BAKER, *passed to* CHARLIE, *passed to* EASY,
who places it on top of the planks. EASY *shouts.*)
Slab!

(*A second slab is thrown in and passed to* EASY *who places it. A
third slab likewise reaches* EASY. *He needs four for his
construction. He shouts.*)
Slab!

(*A block is thrown to* BAKER, *passed to* CHARLIE, *passed to*
EASY, *who impatiently passes it back to* CHARLIE *who passes it
back to* BAKER *who takes it upstage.* EASY *shouts.*)
Slab!

(*Another block is thrown, straight to* CHARLIE *who passes it to*
EASY *who passes it back to* CHARLIE *who walks upstage with it
and places it on the floor.*)
Slab!

ABEL: (*Enters smiling.*) Slab?

EASY: Nit!

ABEL: Nit?

EASY: Git! Slab.

(ABEL *leaves and a moment later another block comes flying
across to* EASY *who catches it, throws it furiously at* BAKER *and*
CHARLIE, *who catch it and put it down.* EASY *walks off into the
wings.*

From his satchel CHARLIE *produces a small transistor radio
which he turns on. He is lucky enough to catch his favourite
song, half-way through the first verse, which we have already
heard.* CHARLIE *sings.*)

EASY: (*Off-stage.*) Useless.

ABEL: *(Politely, off-stage.)* Useless, git.

> *(There is the sound of a slap and a sharp cry from ABEL. EASY re-enters carrying a slab. DOGG now re-enters with a tray of button-holes. He puts this down and picks up the box of flags.)*

DOGG: *(Calling off-stage to ABEL.)* Abel!

ABEL: Slab, git.

DOGG: Brick.

> *(ABEL enters, holding his ear and glancing aggrievedly at EASY. DOGG starts handing out the flags, starting with ABEL, who on receiving his flag goes back off-stage. DOGG hands flags to BAKER, CHARLIE and some of the audience, counting the flags as he gives them out.)*

Sun, dock, trog, slack, pan, sock, slight, bright, none, tun, what, dunce . . .

> *(EASY, who has placed the slab and is watching DOGG, takes a step towards him.)*

EASY: What?

> *(DOGG takes this as a correction.)*

DOGG: Dunce.

EASY: What??

DOGG: Dunce!

EASY: What??

> *(DOGG irritably does a re-count, aloud, and finds that he was right . . .)*

DOGG: Sun, dock, trog, slack, pan, sock, slight, bright, none, tun, what, *dunce*!

EASY: Oh!

DOGG: *(Witheringly.)* Pax!

> *(DOGG then turns his attention to the button-holes. EASY expects to be given one.)*
>
> *(To EASY.)* Nit!
>
> *(He gives a button-hole to CHARLIE.)*

CHARLIE: Cube, git.

DOGG: Block. [*Next.]

> *(BAKER comes forward and receives his button-hole.)*

BAKER: Cube, git.

DOGG: *(Calls out to ABEL.)* Block! Abel!

> *(ABEL comes on and receives his button-hole. ABEL is holding his*

ear in an aggrieved manner, looking at EASY.)

ABEL: Cube, git.

(ABEL *retires back to the lorry.* DOGG *looks expectantly at* EASY.)

DOGG: Slab? [*Okay?]

EASY: Block.

DOGG: Slab.

EASY: Block.

DOGG: Slab.

(*He obviously expects* EASY *to carry on with the work.* EASY
*re-examines the plan, replaces it in his pocket and nervously
calls out to* ABEL.)

EASY: Block!

(*To his surprise and relief a block is thrown in. By this time*
CHARLIE, *who had guiltily turned off the radio as soon as*
DOGG *entered, has gone back to his receiving position, as has*
BAKER. *The block is passed down the line to* EASY *who places it
on top of the slabs. He calls out.*)

Block!

(*Another block follows the same route.* DOGG *leaves satisfied.*
EASY *calls out.*)

Block!

(*A slab is heaved on.* BAKER *catches it and passes it to*
CHARLIE *who, however, anticipates* EASY's *reaction and takes
it back upstage to join the blocks on the floor.* EASY *shouts out.*)

Block!

(*Another slab is heaved on and* BAKER *no less astutely takes it
upstage.* EASY *marches off towards* ABEL.)

CHARLIE: Cretin is he?

BAKER: Cretin is he?—Trog—taxi—marmalade. [*Marmalade
denotes pleasure and approval.]

EASY: (*Off-stage.*) Great Oaf!

ABEL: Git?

(*This is followed by another cry of pain from* ABEL. CHARLIE
*has turned his radio on again. The radio emits the familiar
pips of the time signal.* BAKER *checks his watch.*)

RADIO: Check mumble hardly out. [*Here are the football
results.]

(CHARLIE *takes a pools coupon out of his satchel and starts checking it off. The rhythm of the language coming out of the radio is the familiar one, appropriate to home wins, away wins, and draws.*

The following is a translation of the numbers;

Nil = quite	*3 = trog*
1 = sun	*4 = slack*
2 = dock	*5 = pan*

In addition, 'Clock' and 'Foglamp' correspond to 'City' and 'United'. Thus the result, 'Haddock Clock quite, Haddock Foglamp trog' would be delivered with the inflections appropriate to, say, 'Manchester City nil, Manchester United three'—an away win. The radio starts by saying, 'Oblong Sun' with the inflection of 'Division One'.)

RADIO: Oblong Sun, Dogtrot quite, Flange dock; Cabrank dock, Blanket Clock quite; Tube Clock dock, Handbag dock; Haddock Clock quite, Haddock Foglamp trog; Wonder quite, Picknicking pan . . .

(CHARLIE *whistles at that—a five-nil away win. Meanwhile* EASY *re-enters carrying a tall load of blocks, followed by* ABEL, *limping, carrying a similar load.* EASY *puts his blocks down. He notices the radio and* CHARLIE *checking his pools.* EASY *produces a pools coupon and a pencil before he realizes that he can't make head or tail of the radio.)*

EASY: (*Bemused.*) Do you mind if I ask you something. What wavelength are you on?

(*Meanwhile* BAKER *has started to make a neat wall out of the blocks and slabs which have so far been assembled. It is apparent now that some of the blocks have got apparently random letters printed on them.* EASY, *having put away his pools coupon, adds blocks to the steps.* ABEL *has dumped his load of blocks near* BAKER *and now limps off stage back to the lorry.* DOGG *enters.)*

DOGG: (*To* EASY.) Moronic creep. [*Maroon carpet.*]

(EASY *grabs* DOGG *by the lapel.*)

EASY: Watch it!

(DOGG, *surprised, disengages himself.*)

DOGG: (*To* EASY.) Afternoons—moronic creep?

BAKER: (*To* DOGG.) Brick, git. [*Here, sir.*]

DOGG: Ah. Cube.

(BAKER *points at the carpet.* DOGG *unrolls the red carpet to
make a path from the microphone to the wings.* CHARLIE *has
turned off the radio on* DOGG's *entrance and now* BAKER *rejoins
him in building the wall.* EASY *has completed that stage of the
steps, and the wall is complete.* BAKER *and* CHARLIE *are
nowhere to be seen because they built the wall from the back
and it now conceals them. This leaves* EASY *apparently alone in
front of the wall. He hasn't yet noticed the letters, which read;*

> MATHS
> OLD
> EGG

EASY *takes the plan out of his pocket and studies it again.* DOGG
notices the wall. He looks at EASY. EASY *looks at the wall.*
EASY *looks at* DOGG. EASY *smiles.* DOGG *slaps* EASY *lightly on the
cheek.* EASY *opens his mouth to protest.* DOGG *cuffs him heavily
on the other cheek and knocks* EASY *through the wall which
disintegrates.* DOGG *takes the piece of paper out of* EASY's
pocket and looks at it carefully. EASY *picks himself up.* CHARLIE
and BAKER *go back into their receiving positions.* DOGG *gives
the paper back to* EASY.)

EASY: Here, what's your game?

DOGG: Cube. [*Thank you.]

EASY: Eh?

DOGG: Cube.

(*Then he calls out to* ABEL.)

Cube! Abel!

(*A cube is thrown in to* BAKER, *passed to* CHARLIE, *passed to*
EASY *who puts it in place.* DOGG *to* CHARLIE *and* BAKER.) Slab?

EASY: Cube.

DOGG: Slab.

CHARLIE/BAKER: Cube, git!

EASY: (*With venom.*) Git!

(DOGG *is pleased and smiles.* EASY *is completely at a loss.* DOGG
leaves satisfied.)

Cube!

(*Another cube follows the same route.*)

Cube!

(*A slab sails on and* BAKER *and* CHARLIE *catch it together. They immediately take it upstage and place it down to form the base of a rebuilt wall. They start rebuilding the wall. Meanwhile* EASY *walks off towards* ABEL *and as soon as he is off-stage there is the sound of a thump and a cry from* ABEL. ABEL *walks on, limping, holding his ear and rubbing his backside.*)

EASY: (*Off-stage.*) Cube!

(*A cube sails on over* ABEL's *head, and* ABEL, *who is caught by surprise, catches it and places it on the steps. This keeps happening again and again while* BAKER *and* CHARLIE *rebuild the wall.* ABEL, *however, makes a tower out of the cubes instead of laying them to make a new level. After seven cubes, in toto,* EASY *enters and sees the tottering tower of cubes and just saves them from collapsing.* BAKER *and* CHARLIE *meanwhile have removed themselves from view by rebuilding the wall which now says;*

MEG

SHOT

GLAD

DOGG *enters, carrying a small table with silver trophies covered with a velvet cloth. He walks to the microphone and tests it.*)

DOGG: Sun, dock, trogg . . .

(*The microphone is dead.* DOGG *to* BAKER.)

Haddock priest.

BAKER: Haddock, git?

DOGG: Priest.

(BAKER *goes to the microphone and turns the switch on.*)

Sun, dock, trog . . . Gymshoes. [*Excellent.]

(*The microphone is live. Meanwhile* EASY *has placed all the cubes correctly so that they make a top layer to the steps. He is one cube short, however.* ABEL *goes back to the lorry.*)

EASY: Cube short.

DOGG: (*To* EASY.) Brick?

EASY: Cube!

DOGG: Brick.

EASY: Cube!

(*A cube sails in from the lorry and* EASY *catches it and then the steps are complete.* DOGG *turns to go, sees the new wall with its*

message and looks at EASY. EASY *looks at the wall. He looks at*
DOGG.)

Pax!

(DOGG *knocks him through the wall which disintegrates.* DOGG
leaves. CHARLIE *and* BAKER *start re-assembling the components
of the wall.* EASY *shouts after* DOGG.)

Yob! [*Flowers.]

(CHARLIE, BAKER *and* EASY *are roughly in line by the carpet.*
DOGG *reappears immediately with a bouquet which is wrapped
in cellophane and tied with a red ribbon. It is important that it
is distinctive because it appears in the second half of the play.
He hands this to* CHARLIE. *March music is heard.* CHARLIE *gives
the bouquet to* BAKER *who gives it to* EASY *who thrusts it into*
DOGG'*s hands as he exits.* DOGG *re-enters furiously and gives
flowers back to* EASY *who gives them to* ABEL *as he enters.* ABEL
gives them to CHARLIE *who loses them while rebuilding the wall.*
EASY *exits and returns with lid for platform.* CHARLIE *and*
BAKER, *now joined by* ABEL, *rebuild the wall, then take their
little flags out of their pockets and start waving them.* EASY
joins in unhappily.

A LADY *enters followed by a smirking* DOGG. *The music plays,
the flags wave. The* LADY *gets to the microphone. The music
stops and she is ready to give her speech which is written on a
neat postcard held in her gloved hand.*)

LADY: (*Nicely.*) Scabs, slobs, yobs, yids, spicks, wops . . .

(*As one might say Your Grace, ladies and gentlemen, boys and
girls . . .*)

Sad fact, brats pule puke crap-pot stink, spit; grow up
dunces crooks; rank socks dank snotrags, conkers, ticks; crib
books, cock snooks, block bogs, jack off, catch pox pick spots,
scabs, padlocks, seek kicks, kinks, slack; nick swag, swig
coke, bank kickbacks; . . . frankly can't stick kids. Mens sana
in corpore sano.

(*Applause.* LADY *comes down from the platform helped by* DOGG.
They stand by the table. DOGG *lifts the cloth to reveal the
school trophies.*)

DOGG: (*Presenting school prizes reads.*) Pansticks jammy, sun-up—
Fox Major.

(FOX *enters from auditorium left, climbs steps to stage and collects his prize. He shakes hands with a beaming* LADY.)

FOX: Cube, get. [*Thank you, madam.]

(FOX *exits into auditorium right.*)

DOGG: As Grimsby primate what, sun-up—Fox Major.

(FOX, *still near the front of the auditorium, turns and awkwardly squeezes in between two rows of seats. As he steps over the audience's legs he apologetically exclaims 'Cutlery' [*Excuse me], reaches stage and receives prize as before.*)

Cuff-laces empty cross . . . Crazy jogs . . . Poodle-fire . . . Melon legs arc lamps . . . pelvic wiggle stamp . . . grinning . . . grape-soot pergolas . . . fairly pricks double . . . elegant frantically . . . plugs . . . Fox Major.

(DOGG *has been placing all these trophies on top of the velvet which covered them earlier, and which he has placed on the platform* EASY *built.* FOX *whoops when he hears his name and rushes onto the stage as before, but picks up the table, which is now quite bare, and exits trimphantly stage left.*

Throughout this presentation ABLE, BAKER *and* CHARLIE *have been waving their flags each time* FOX *arrives on stage, but their faces reveal their dissatisfaction and boredom.*)

Practically . . . Helmet bedsocks Denmark. [*And now . . . Helmet Prince of Denmark.]

MRS DOGG (*Correcting him.*) Hamlet . . .

DOGG: Hamlet bedsocks Denmark, yeti William Shakespeare. (*To* MRS DOGG.) Yob?

MRS DOGG: Yob . . . yob . . . yob? [*Flowers?]

(*She looks to schoolboys, who know nothing of their whereabouts.* MRS DOGG *turns away and gives* LADY *her button-hole, with a little curtsey. To* LADY.)

Hernia, suppurating kidneys, reeks cat-boils frankly gangrenous armpit dripping maggots . . .

LADY: (*With energy and charm.*) Sod the pudding club!

(*Music.* DOGG, MRS DOGG *and* LADY *begin to exit past the wall. The* LADY *notices the message on the wall which says:*

GOD
SLAG
THEM

She is taken aback but bravely continues out. DOGG *looks daggers at* EASY. *As soon as the* LADY *and* MRS DOGG *have left the stage* DOGG *does an about-turn and marches back to* EASY. EASY *looks at* DOGG. DOGG *looks at the wall.* EASY *dutifully hurls himself through the wall which disintegrates.* DOGG *leaves.* EASY *picks himself up. He shouts furiously after* DOGG.)

EASY: Stinkbag! Poxy crank!

(ABEL, BAKER *and* CHARLIE *are also resentful about* DOGG *and all their succeeding lines, as are* EASY's, *are insults referring to* DOGG, *though not necessarily called out after him.*)

BAKER: Pax! Quinces carparks!

EASY: Canting poncey creep!

CHARLIE: Daisy squire!

EASY: Sadist! Fascist!

ABEL: Fishes! Afternoons!

EASY: Officious bastard! Lunatic!

ABEL: Avacados castle sofa Dogg!

EASY: Have his guts for garters, see if I don't!

ABEL: (*Talking to* EASY *about* DOGG.) Avocados castle cigar smoke.

EASY: (*To* ABLE.) Right!—See if I don't! Kick his backside!

BAKER: (*To* EASY.) Quinces ice-packs!

EASY: (*To* BAKER.) Right!

CHARLIE: Daisy squire!

BAKER: Slab git, nit git—

EASY: Three bags full git! Crazy little squirt!

CHARLIE: Daisy vanilla!

EASY: Squire! Quince bog! Have his pax for carpox—so help me Dogg, see avocado!——Slab.

BAKER: Moronic creep.

EASY: Slab. Cretinous pig-face?

BAKER: Cretinous pig-face? Slack-dunce. [*4: 10.]

EASY: What?

BAKER: Dunce.

EASY: Cube.

(*During the above* ABEL, BAKER *and* CHARLIE *have been rebuilding the wall, and* EASY *has been rolling up the red carpet. Now* EASY *starts collecting all the flags back starting with the three flags given to* ABEL, BAKER *and* CHARLIE *which*

*they threw to the floor in disgust. He collects flags from the
audience and counts them as he collects them, and thanks each
one, 'Cube', as he does so.)*
Sun, dock, trog, slack, pan, sock, slight, bright, none, fun,
what, dunce!
(ABEL, BAKER *and* CHARLIE *have just finished building the wall
and have built themselves out of view.* EASY *moves to exit, when
we hear . . .)*

BAKER: (*From behind screen and pointing at microphone.*) Haddock.
(EASY *returns and takes off microphone. Before he exits . . .)*

EASY: Hamlet bedsocks Denmark. Yeti William Shakespeare.
(*The wall says:*

DOGGS
HAM
LET

The lighting changes and there is a trumpet fanfare and DOGG
enters now dressed to take his part in the 15-*Minute Hamlet.
He goes to the platform, from which he speaks the prologue of
the* Hamlet, *and then exits. This leaves the wall and the steps
to be used as the walls and ramparts of Elsinore. At the back
of the stage left and right are two folding screens. The stage
left screen has a bolt through the top which allows a cut-out
sun, moon and crown to be swung into vision from behind the
screen. From the on-stage side pivots a two-dimensional cut-out
grave for* OPHELIA.)

PROLOGUE

Enter SHAKESPEARE, *bows.*
SHAKESPEARE: For this relief, much thanks.
        Though I am native here, and to the manner born,
        It is a custom more honoured in the breach
        Than in the observance
        Well.
        Something is rotten in the state of Denmark.
        To be, or not to be, that is the question.
        There are more things in heaven and earth
        Than are dreamt of in your philosophy—

There's a divinity that shapes our ends,
Rough hew them how we will
Though this be madness, yet there is method in it.
I must be cruel only to be kind;
Hold, as t'were, the mirror up to nature.
A countenance more in sorrow than in anger.
(LADY *in audience shouts* 'Marmalade'.)
The lady doth protest too much.
Cat will mew, and Dogg will have his day!
(*Bows and exits. End of prologue.*)

A castle battlement. Thunder and wind. Enter two GUARDS: BERNARDO/
MARCELLUS *and* FRANCISCO/HORATIO. *The* GUARDS *are played by* ABEL
and BAKER *respectively. They are costumed for a typical Shakespeare
play except that they have short trousers.* GUARDS *on the platform.*

BERNARDO: Who's there?

FRANCISCO: Nay, answer me.

BERNARDO: Long live the King. Get thee to bed.

FRANCISCO: For this relief, much thanks.

BERNARDO: What, has this thing appeared again tonight?

FRANCISCO: Peace, break thee off: look where it comes again!

BERNARDO: Looks it not like the King?

FRANCISCO: By heaven, I charge thee, speak!

BERNARDO: (*Points and looks left.*) 'Tis here.

FRANCISCO: (*Points and looks right.*) 'Tis there.

BERNARDO: (*Looks right.*) 'Tis gone.

FRANCISCO: But look, the morn in russet mantle clad
Walks o'er the dew of yon high eastern hill.
(*On 'But look' a cut-out sun shoots up over the stage
left screen, and descends here.*)

BERNARDO: Let us impart what we have seen tonight
Unto young Hamlet.
(*Exeunt. End scene.*)

*A room of state within the castle. A cut-out crown hinges over stage
left screen.*

Flourish of trumpets. Enter CLAUDIUS *and* GERTRUDE, *who is played by* MRS DOGG.

  CLAUDIUS: Though yet of Hamlet our dear brother's death
               The memory be green
               (*Enter* HAMLET *who is played by* FOX MAJOR.)
               Our sometime sister, now our Queen
               Have we taken to wife.
               But now, my cousin Hamlet, and my son—
  HAMLET: A little more than kin, and less than kind.
               (*Exit* CLAUDIUS *and* GERTRUDE.)
               O that this too too solid flesh would melt!
               That it should come to this—but two months dead!
               So loving to my mother: Frailty, thy name is
                 woman!
               Married with mine uncle, my father's brother.
               The funeral baked meats did coldly furnish forth
               The marriage tables.
               (*The crown hinges down.* HORATIO *rushes on.*)
  HORATIO: My lord, I think I saw him yesternight—
               The King, your father—upon the platform where
                 we watched.
  HAMLET: 'Tis very strange.
  HORATIO: Armed, my lord—
               A countenance more in sorrow than in anger.
  HAMLET: My father's spirit in arms? All is not well.
               Would the night were come!
               (*The moon hinges up. Exeunt to parapet. End scene.*)

The castle battlements at night. Noise of carouse, cannon, fireworks.
  HORATIO *and* HAMLET *appear on platform built by* EASY.
  HAMLET: The King doth wake tonight and takes his rouse,
               Though I am native here and to the manner born,
               It is a custom more honoured in the breach
               Than in the observance.
               (*Wind noise.*)
  HORATIO: Look, my lord, it comes. (*Points*)
               (*Enter* GHOST *above the wall built of blocks.*)

HAMLET: Angels and ministers of grace defend us!
        Something is rotten in the state of Denmark!
        Alas, poor ghost.

GHOST: I am thy father's spirit.
        Revenge his foul and most unnnatural murder.

HAMLET: Murder?

GHOST: The serpent that did sting thy father's life
        Now wears his crown.

HAMLET: O my prophetic soul? Mine uncle?
        (*Exit* GHOST. *To* HORATIO.)
        There are more things in heaven and earth
        Than are dreamt of in your philosophy.
        (*Exit* HORATIO.)
        Hereafter I shall think meet
        To put an antic disposition on.
        The time is out of joint. O cursed spite
        That ever I was born to set it right!
        (*Exit* HAMLET. *Moon hinges down. End scene.*)

A room within. Crown hinges up. Flourish of trumpets leading into flute and harpsichord music. Enter POLONIUS; OPHELIA *rushes on.* OPHELIA *is, of course, played by* CHARLIE.

POLONIUS: How now Ophelia, what's the matter?

OPHELIA: My lord, as I was sewing in my chamber,
        Lord Hamlet with his doublet all unbraced;
        No hat upon his head, pale as his shirt,
        His knees knocking each other, and with a look so
            piteous
        He comes before me.

POLONIUS: Mad for thy love?
        I have found the very cause of Hamlet's lunacy.
        (*Enter* HAMLET, *exit* OPHELIA.)
        Look where sadly the poor wretch comes reading
        What do you read, my lord?

HAMLET: Words, words, words.

POLONIUS: Though this be madness, yet there is method in it.

HAMLET: I am but mad north northwest: when the wind is

southerly I know a hawk from a
handsaw.
(*Slams book shut and against* POLONIUS's *chest.*)

POLONIUS: The actors are come hither, my lord. (*Exits*)

HAMLET: We'll hear a play tomorrow.
I have heard that guilty creatures sitting at a play
Have by the very cunning of the scene
Been struck so to the soul that presently
They have proclaimed their malefactions.
I'll have these players play something
Like the murder of my father before mine uncle.
If he but blench, I know my course.
The play's the thing
Wherein I'll catch the conscience of the King.
(*Pause*)
To be, or not to be (*Puts dagger, pulled from his
sleeve, to heart.
Enter* CLAUDIUS *and* OPHELIA.)
that is the question.

OPHELIA: My lord—

HAMLET: Get thee to a nunnery!
(*Exit* OPHELIA *and* HAMLET.)

CLAUDIUS: Love? His affections do not that way tend
There's something in his soul
O'er which his melancholy sits on brood.
He shall with speed to England.
(*Exit* CLAUDIUS. *End scene.*)

A hall within the castle. Flourish of trumpets. Enter HAMLET *and*
OPHELIA, MARCELLUS *and* HORATIO *joking,* CLAUDIUS *and* GERTRUDE.
Puppet players appear above stage left screen.

HAMLET: (*To puppet players.*) Speak the speech, I pray you, as I
pronounced it to you; trippingly on the tongue.
Hold, as t'were, the mirror up to nature
(ALL *sit to watch puppet play. Masque music*)
(*To* GERTRUDE.) Madam, how like you the play?

GERTRUDE: The lady doth protest too much, methinks.

HAMLET: He poisons him in the garden of his estate. You
        shall see anon how the murderer gets the love of
        Gonzago's wife.
        (CLAUDIUS *rises*.)
        The King rises!
        (*Music stops, hubbub noise starts.*)
        What, frighted with false fire?
        (*Exit,* CLAUDIUS.)

ALL: Give o'er the play.
        (*Puppets disappear, crown disappears.*)

HAMLET: Lights! Lights! Lights! I'll take the ghost's word
        for a thousand pounds!
        (*Exeunt* ALL *except* POLONIUS.)

POLONIUS: (*Standing at side.*) He's going to his mother's closet.
        Behind the arras I'll convey myself to hear the
        process.
        (*End scene.*)

The Queen's apartment. POLONIUS *stands by stage right screen and
hinges a curtain out from behind it. Lute music. Enter* HAMLET *and*
GERTRUDE.

HAMLET: Now Mother, what's the matter?

GERTRUDE: Hamlet, thou hast thy father much offended.

HAMLET: Mother, you have my father much offended.
        (*Holds her.*)

GERTRUDE: What wilt thou do? Thou wilt not murder me?
        Help! Help! Ho!

POLONIUS: (*Behind the arras.*) Help!

HAMLET: How now? A rat? (*Stabs* POLONIUS.) Dead for a
        ducat, dead!

GERTRUDE: O me, what hast thou done?

HAMLET: Nay, I know not.

GERTRUDE: Alas, he's mad.

HAMLET: I must be cruel only to be kind. Good night,
        Mother.
        (*Exit* HAMLET *dragging* POLONIUS. *Exit* GERTRUDE,
        sobbing. Arras hinges back. End scene.)

*Another room in the castle. Flourish of trumpets. Crown hinges up.
Enter* CLAUDIUS *and* HAMLET.

CLAUDIUS: Now, Hamlet, where's Polonius?

HAMLET: At supper. (*Hiding his sword clumsily.*)

CLAUDIUS: Hamlet, this deed must send thee hence.
           Therefore prepare thyself,
           Everything is bent for England.
           (*Exit* HAMLET.)
           And England, if my love thou holds't at aught,
           Thou may'st not coldly set our sov'reign process,
           The present death of Hamlet. Do it, England!
           (*Exit* CLAUDIUS. *Crown hingest down. End scene.*)

At sea.
Sea music. A sail appears above stage left screen. Enter HAMLET *on
platform, swaying as if on ship's bridge. He wipes his eyes, and becomes
seasick. End sea music. Exit* HAMLET, *holding his hand to his mouth.*

Yet another room in the castle. Flourish of trumpets. Enter CLAUDIUS
and LAERTES.

LAERTES: Where is my father?

CLAUDIUS: Dead.
    (*Enter* OPHELIA *in mad trance, singing and carrying a bouquet
    of flowers wrapped in cellophane and with a red ribbon. Lute
    music.*)

OPHELIA: They bore him barefaced on the bier,
           (*After her first line she gives a flower to* LAERTES.)
           Hey nonny nonny, hey nonny.
           (*After her second, she slams the bouquet in* CLAUDIUS's
           *stomach. It is, of course, the missing bouquet from the
           speech-day ceremony.*)

OPHELIA: And on his grave rained many a tear . . .
           (*Half-way through her third line she disappears behind
           the screen stage left and pauses.* CLAUDIUS *and* LAERTES
           *peer round the side she disappeared and she runs round
           the other behind them.*)

LAERTES: O heat dry up my brains—O kind Sister,
(OPHELIA *falls to ground. She catches a flower thrown from stage right screen.*)
Had'st thou thy wits, and did'st persuade revenge
It could not move thus.

CLAUDIUS: And where the offence is, let the great axe fall.
(*Exit* CLAUDIUS *and* LAERTES. OPHELIA *sits up to reach gravestone which she swings down to conceal her. Bell tolls four times. End scene.*)

A churchyard. Enter GRAVEDIGGER *and* HAMLET.

HAMLET: Ere we were two days at sea, a pirate of very warlike appointment gave us chase. In the grapple I boarded them. On the instant they got clear of our ship; so I alone became their prisoner. They have dealt with me like thieves of mercy.

GRAVEDIGGER: What is he that builds stronger than either the mason, the shipwright or the carpenter?

HAMLET: A gravemaker. The houses he makes will last till Doomsday.
(GRAVEDIGGER *gives skull to* HAMLET.)
Whose was it?

GRAVEDIGGER: This same skull, Sir, was Yorick's skull, the King's jester.

HAMLET: Alas, poor Yorick. (*Returns skull to* GRAVEDIGGER.)
But soft—that is Laertes. (*Withdraws to side.*)
(*Enter* LAERTES.)

LAERTES: What ceremony else?
Lay her in the earth,
May violets spring. I tell thee, churlish priest . . .
(*Enter* CLAUDIUS *and* GERTRUDE.)
A ministering angel shall my sister be
When thou liest howling.

HAMLET: (*Hiding behind the brick platform.*) What, the fair Ophelia?

LAERTES: O treble woe. Hold off the earth awhile,
Till I have caught her once more in my arms.

HAMLET: (*Re-entering acting area.*)
> What is he whose grief bears such an emphasis?
> This is I, Hamlet the Dane!

LAERTES: The devil take thy soul.
> (*They grapple.*)

HAMLET: Away thy hand!
> (CLAUDIUS *and* GERTRUDE *pull them apart.*)

CLAUDIUS/GERTRUDE: Hamlet! Hamlet!

HAMLET: I loved Ophelia. What wilt thou do for her?

GERTRUDE: O he is mad. Laertes!
> (*Exit* CLAUDIUS, GERTRUDE *and* LAERTES.)

HAMLET: The cat will mew, and dog will have his day!
> (*Exeunt. End scene.*)

A hall in the castle. Flourish of trumpets, crown hinges up.
Enter HAMLET.

HAMLET: There's a divinity that shapes our ends, rough hew
> them how we will. But thou would'st not think how
> ill all's here about my heart. But 'tis no matter. We
> defy augury. There is a special providence in the
> fall of a sparrow. If it be now, 'tis not to come; if it
> be not to come, it will be now; if it be not now, yet
> it will come. The readiness is all.
> (LAERTES *enters with* OSRIC *bearing swords followed by*
> CLAUDIUS *and* GERTRUDE *with goblets.*)
> Come on, Sir!

LAERTES: Come, my lord.
> (*Fanfare of trumpets. They draw and duel.*)

HAMLET: One.

LAERTES: No.

HAMLET: Judgement?

OSRIC: A hit, a very palpable hit.

CLAUDIUS: Stay, give me a drink.
> Hamlet, this pearl is thine, here's to thy health.
> (*Drops pearl in goblet.*)
> Give him the cup.

GERTRUDE: The Queen carouses to thy fortune, Hamlet.

CLAUDIUS: Gertrude, do not drink!

GERTRUDE: I will, my lord. (*Drinks*)

LAERTES: My lord, I'll hit him now.
Have at you, now!
(*The grapple and fight.*)

CLAUDIUS: Part them, they are incensed.
They bleed on both sides.
(OSRIC *and* CLAUDIUS *part them.*)

LAERTES: I am justly killed by my own treachery. (*Falls*)

GERTRUDE: The drink, the drink! I am poisoned! (*Dies*)

HAMLET: Treachery! Seek it out.
(*Enter* FORTINBRAS.)

LAERTES: It is here, Hamlet. Hamlet thou art slain.
Lo, here I lie, never to rise again.
The King, the King's to blame.

HAMLET: The point envenomed too?
Then venom to thy work. (*Kills* CLAUDIUS.)
(*Crown hinges down.*)

LAERTES: Exchange forgiveness with me, noble Ha . . . m . . .
(*Dies*)

HAMLET: I follow thee.
I cannot live to hear the news from England.
The rest is silence. (*Dies*)

HORATIO: Good night sweet prince,
And flights of angels sing thee to thy rest.
(*Turns to face away from audience.*)
Go, bid the soldiers shoot.
(*Four shots heard from off-stage.* ALL *stand, bow once
and exit. End.*)

THE ENCORE

*Encore signs appear above each screen. Flourish of trumpets, crown
hinges up. Enter* CLAUDIUS *and* GERTRUDE.

CLAUDIUS: Our sometime sister, now our Queen,
(*Enter* HAMLET.)
Have we taken to wife.

(Crown hinges down.)

HAMLET: That it should come to this!
(Exit CLAUDIUS *and* GERTRUDE. *Wind noise. Moon hinges up. Enter* HORATIO *above.)*

HORATIO: My lord, I saw him yesternight—
The King, your father.

HAMLET: Angels and ministers of grace defend us!
(Exit, running, through rest of speech.)
Something is rotten in the state of Denmark.
(Enter GHOST *above.)*

GHOST: I am thy father's spirit.
The serpent that did sting thy father's life
(Enter HAMLET *above.)*
Now wears his crown.

HAMLET: O my prophetic soul!
Hereafter I shall think meet
To put an antic disposition on.
*(Moon hinges down. Exeunt.
Short flourish of trumpets. Enter* POLONIUS *below, running. Crown hinges up.)*

POLONIUS: Look where sadly the poor wretch comes.
(Exit POLONIUS, *running. Enter* HAMLET.)*

HAMLET: I have heard that guilty creatures sitting at a play
Have by the very cunning of the scene been struck.
(Enter CLAUDIUS, GERTRUDE, OPHELIA, MARCELLUS *and* HORATIO *joking.* ALL *sit to watch imaginary play, puppets appear above screen.)*
If he but blench, I know my course.
(Masque music. CLAUDIUS *rises.)*
The King rises!

ALL: Give o'er the play!
(Exeunt ALL *except* GERTRUDE *and* HAMLET. *Crown hinges down.)*

HAMLET: I'll take the ghost's word for a thousand pounds.
(Enter POLONIUS, *goes behind arras. Short flourish of trumpets.)*
Mother, you have my father much offended.

GERTRUDE: Help!

POLONIUS: Help, Ho!

HAMLET: (*Stabs* POLONIUS.) Dead for a ducat, dead!
(POLONIUS *falls dead off-stage. Exit* GERTRUDE *and*
HAMLET. *Short flourish of trumpets. Enter* CLAUDIUS
followed by HAMLET.)

CLAUDIUS: Hamlet, this deed must send thee hence
(*Exit* HAMLET.)
Do it, England.
(*Exit* CLAUDIUS. *Enter* OPHELIA, *falls to ground. Rises
and pulls gravestone to cover herself. Bell tolls twice.
Enter* GRAVEDIGGER *and* HAMLET.)

HAMLET: A pirate gave us chase. I alone became their prisoner.
(*Takes skull from* GRAVEDIGGER.)
Alas poor Yorick—but soft (*Returns skull to*
GRAVEDIGGER.)—This is I,
Hamlet the Dane!
(*Exit* GRAVEDIGGER. *Enter* LAERTES.)

LAERTES: The devil take thy soul!
(*They grapple, then break. Enter* OSRIC *between them
with swords. They draw. Crown hinges up. Enter*
CLAUDIUS *and* GERTRUDE *with goblets.*)

HAMLET: Come on, Sir!
(LAERTES *and* HAMLET *fight.*)

OSRIC: A hit, a very palpable hit!

CLAUDIUS: Give him the cup. Gertrude, do not drink!

GERTRUDE: I am poisoned! (*Dies*)

LAERTES: Hamlet, thou art slain! (*Dies*)

HAMLET: Then venom to thy work! (*Kills* CLAUDIUS.
Crown hinges down.)
The rest is silence. (*Dies*)
(*Two shots off-stage. End*)

The actors stand up to take their curtain call. While this is going on
EASY *walks on whistling, lifts lid from steps, removes a cube and walks
off with it. The actors retire.*

EASY: (*To audience.*) Cube . . .
(*He walks out.*)

CAHOOT'S MACBETH

Cahoot's Macbeth is
dedicated to
the Czechoslovakian playwright
Pavel Kohout

CHARACTERS

MACBETH
LADY MACBETH
BANQUO
MACDUFF
ROSS
DUNCAN
MALCOLM
1ST WITCH
2ND WITCH
3RD WITCH
1ST MURDERER
2ND MURDERER
LENNOX
MESSENGER
CAHOOT
INSPECTOR
HOSTESS
EASY
POLICEMAN

Guests, Voices, Child's Voice

The shortened *Macbeth* has not been organized for any specific number of actors. Ideally it would be done without much in the way of doubling, but it may be done with a minimum of three male and two female actors. In the Czech productions, Kohout distributed the roles as follows (I have not used Donalbain, Wounded Captain, Macduff's wife, or a second messenger):

FIRST ACTOR	Macbeth
SECOND ACTOR	Duncan, Banquo, Macduff, 1st Murderer, Messenger
THIRD ACTOR	Ross, Malcolm, 2nd Murderer, 3rd Witch
FIRST ACTRESS	2nd Witch, Servant
SECOND ACTRESS	Lady Macbeth, 1st Witch

The action takes place in the living room of a flat.
Thunder and lightning. Three WITCHES *in minimal light.*

1ST WITCH: When shall we three meet again?
In thunder, lightning, or in rain?

2ND WITCH: When the hurly-burly's done,
When the battle's lost and won.

3RD WITCH: That will be ere the set of sun.

1ST WITCH: Where the place?

2ND WITCH: Upon the heath.

3RD WITCH: There to meet with Macbeth.

ALL: Fair is foul, and foul is fair.
Hover through the fog and filthy air.
(*Four drum beats.*)

3RD WITCH: A drum! a drum!
Macbeth doth come.
(*Enter* MACBETH *and* BANQUO.)

MACBETH: So foul and fair a day I have not seen.

BANQUO: How far is't called to Forres? What are these, so
withered and so wild in their attire, That look
not like the inhabitants o'the earth, And yet are
on't?

MACBETH: Speak if you can! What are you?
(*The* WITCHES *encircle* MACBETH.)

1ST WITCH: All hail, Macbeth! Hail to thee, Thane of
Glamis!

2ND WITCH: All hail, Macbeth! Hail to thee, Thane of
Cawdor!

3RD WITCH: All hail, Macbeth, that shalt be king hereafter!

BANQUO: Speak then to me who neither beg nor fear
Your favours nor your hate.

3RD WITCH: Thou shalt get kings, though thou be none.
So all hail, Macbeth and Banquo!

1ST WITCH: Banquo and Macbeth, all hail!
(*The* WITCHES *vanish.*)

MACBETH: Stay, you imperfect speakers! Tell me more!

BANQUO: Wither are they vanished?
(*Lights up to reveal living room.*)

MACBETH: Into the air;
Would they had stayed!

BANQUO: Were such things here as we do speak about?
Or have we eaten on the insane root
That takes the reason prisoner?

MACBETH: Your children shall be kings.

BANQUO: You shall be king.

MACBETH: And Thane of Cawdor too, went it not so?

BANQUO: To the selfsame tune and words.
(*Enter* ROSS.)
Who's there?

ROSS: The King hath happily received, Macbeth,
The news of thy success. I am sent
To give thee from our royal master thanks;
And for an earnest of a greater honour,
He bade me from him call thee Thane of
Cawdor.

BANQUO: What! Can the devil speak true?

MACBETH: The Thane of Cawdor lives. Why do you dress
me
In borrowed robes?

ROSS: Who was the Thane lives yet;
But treasons capital, confessed, and proved
Have overthrown him.
(ROSS *hands* MACBETH *a chain and seal which were
Cawdor's.*)

MACBETH: (*Aside*) Glamis, and Thane of Cawdor!
The greatest is behind. Two truths are told
As happy prologues to the swelling Act
Of the imperial theme—I thank you, gentlemen.

ROSS: My worthy Cawdor!

(*Exit* ROSS *and* BANQUO.)

MACBETH: (*Aside*) Stars hide your fires,
Let not light see my black and deep desires.
(*Exit* MACBETH.
Drums.
Enter LADY MACBETH *reading a letter.*)

LADY MACBETH: (*Reading aloud to herself.*) 'Whiles I stood rapt in
the wonder of it, came missives from the King,
who all-hailed me, "Thane of Cawdor"; by
which title, before, these weird sisters saluted me,
and referred me to the coming on of time, with
"Hail, king that shalt be." This have I thought
good to deliver thee, my dearest partner of
greatness, that thou mightest not lose the dues of
rejoicing by being ignorant of what greatness is
promised thee. Lay it to thy heart, and farewell.'
Glamis thou art, and Cawdor; and shalt be
What thou art promised. Yet do I fear thy
    nature:
It is too full o'the milk of human kindness,
To catch the nearest way. Hie thee hither,
That I may pour my spirits in thine ear,
And chastise with the valour of my tongue
All that impedes thee from the golden round,
Which fate and metaphysical aid doth seem
To have thee crowned withal.
(*Enter* IST MESSENGER.)
What is your tidings?

MESSENGER: The king comes here tonight.

LADY MACBETH: Thou'rt mad to say it!
Is not thy master with him?

MESSENGER: Our Thane is coming;
One of my fellows had the speed of him.

LADY MACBETH: He brings great news.
(*Exit* IST MESSENGER.)
The raven himself is hoarse
That croaks the fatal entrance of Duncan
Under my battlements. Come, you spirits

That tend on mortal thoughts, unsex me here
And fill me, from the crown to the toe, top-full
Of direst cruelty.
(*Enter* MACBETH.)
Great Glamis, worthy Cawdor!
Greater than both by the all-hail hereafter!
(*They embrace.*)

MACBETH: Duncan comes here tonight.

LADY MACBETH: And when goes hence?

MACBETH: Tomorrow, as he purposes.

LADY MACBETH: O never
Shall sun that morrow see! Look like the
    innocent flower,
But be the serpent under't.
(*Voices heard off-stage.*)
He that's coming
Must be provided for—

MACBETH: We will speak further. (*He goes to door stage
right.* DUNCAN *is approaching, accompanied by*
BANQUO *and* ROSS, *and by two Gatecrashers,
uniformed policemen, who proceed to investigate
actors and audience with their flashlights before
disappearing into the wings.*)

DUNCAN: This castle hath a pleasant seat; the air
Nimbly and sweetly recommends itself
Unto our gentle senses.
(LADY MACBETH *goes to meet him.*)
See, see, our honoured hostess—
(LADY MACBETH *gives a curtsey.*)
Where's the Thane of Cawdor?

MACBETH: (*Re-entering from threshold.*) Your servant.
(MACBETH *steps forward and bows.*)

DUNCAN: (*To* LADY MACBETH.) Fair and noble hostess, we
are your guest tonight.
Give me your hand.
(LADY MACBETH *leads him out followed by* ROSS
and BANQUO. MACBETH *remains.*)

MACBETH: If it were done, when 'tis done, then 'twere well
It were done quickly. He's here in double trust:

First, as I am his kinsman and his subject,
Strong both against the deed; then, as his host,
Who should against his murderer shut the door,
Not bear the knife myself. I have no spur
To prick the sides of my intent, but only
Vaulting ambition, which o'erleaps itself
And falls on the other.
(*Enter* LADY MACBETH.)
How now? What news? Hath he asked for me?

LADY MACBETH: Know you not he has?

MACBETH: We will proceed no further in this business.

LADY MACBETH: And live a coward in thine own esteem,
Letting 'I dare not' wait upon 'I would',
Like the poor cat i' the adage?
But screw your courage to the sticking place,
And we'll not fail. When Duncan is asleep—
What cannot you and I perform upon
The unguarded Duncan?
(BANQUO *is approaching.*)

MACBETH: (*Off-stage*) Who's there?
MACBETH *goes to meet him at window,* LADY
MACBETH *behind.*)

BANQUO: (*From window.*) A friend.
What, sir, not yet at rest? The King's a-bed.
I dreamt last night of the three sisters.
To you they have showed some truth.

MACBETH: I think not of them. Good repose the while.

BANQUO: Thanks, sir; the like to you.
(MACBETH *closes shutters.*)

MACBETH: Is this a dagger which I see before me,
The handle towards my hand? Come, let me
clutch thee—
I have thee not and yet I see thee still!
(*A bell sounds.*)
I go, and it is done; the bell invites me.
Hear it not, Duncan, for it is a knell
That summons thee to heaven or to hell.
(*Exit* MACBETH. *Sounds of owls and crickets. Enter*
LADY MACBETH *holding a goblet.*)

LADY MACBETH: That which hath made them drunk hath made
    me bold;
The doors are open, and the surfeited grooms
Do mock their charge with snores; I have
    drugged their possets.
(*Owl and crickets.*)
I laid their daggers ready.
Had he not resembled
My father as he slept, I had done't.
(*Enter* MACBETH *carrying two blood-stained
daggers.*)
My husband!

MACBETH: I have done the deed. Didst thou not hear a
noise?

LADY MACBETH: I heard the owl scream and the crickets cry.
(*A police siren is heard approaching the house.
During the following dialogue the car arrives and
the car doors are heard to slam.*)

MACBETH: There's one did laugh in 's sleep, and one cried
    'Murder!'
One cried 'God bless us!' and 'Amen' the other,
(*Siren stops.*)
As they had seen me with these hangman's hands.

LADY MACBETH: Consider it not so deeply.
These deeds must not be thought
After these ways; so, it will make us mad.

MACBETH: Methought I heard a voice cry, 'Sleep no more!
Macbeth does murder sleep'—
(*Sharp rapping.*)
Whence is that knocking?
(*Sharp rapping.*)
How is't with me when every noise appals me?

LADY MACBETH: My hands are of your colour; but I shame
To wear a heart so white.
Retire we to our chamber.

MACBETH: Wake Duncan with thy knocking! (*Sharp
    rapping.*)
I would thou couldst!

(They leave. The knocking off-stage continues. A door, off-stage, opens and closes. The door into the room opens and the INSPECTOR *enters an empty room. He seems surprised to find himself where he is. He affects a sarcastic politeness.)*

INSPECTOR: Oh—I'm sorry—is this the National Theatre?

(A woman, the HOSTESS, *approaches through the audience.)*

HOSTESS: No.

INSPECTOR: It isn't? Wait a minute—I could have made a mistake . . . is it the National Academy of Dramatic Art, or, as we say down Mexico way, NADA? . . . No? I'm utterly nonplussed. I must have got my wires crossed somewhere. *(He is wandering around the room, looking at the walls and ceiling.)*

Testing, testing—one, two, three . . .

(To the ceiling. In other words the room is bugged for sound.)

Is it the home of the Bohemian Light Opera?

HOSTESS: It's *my* home.

INSPECTOR: *(Surprised)* You live here?

HOSTESS: Yes.

INSPECTOR: Don't you find it rather inconvenient, having a lot of preening exhibitionists projecting their voices around the place?—and that's just the audience. I mean, who wants to be packed out night after night by a crowd of fashionable bronchitics saying 'I don't think it's as good as his last one,' and expecting to use your lavatory at will? Not to mention putting yourself at the mercy of any Tom, Dick or Bertolt who can't universalize our predicament without playing ducks and drakes with your furniture arrangements. I don't know why you put up with it. You've got your rights. *(Nosing around he picks up a tea-cosy to reveal a telephone.)*

You've even got a telephone. I can see you're not at the bottom of the social heap. What do you do?

HOSTESS: I'm an artist.

INSPECTOR: *(Cheerfully)* Well it's not the first time I've been wrong. Is this 'phone practical?

(To ceiling again.) Six seven eight one double one.

(He replaces the receiver.)

Yes, if you had any pride in your home you wouldn't take

standing-room only in your sitting-room lying down.

(*The telephone rings in his hand. He lifts it up.*)

Six seven eight one double one? Clear as a bell. Who do you want?

(*He looks round.*)

Is Roger here?

(*Into the 'phone.*)

Roger who? Roger and out?

(*He removes the 'phone from his ear and frowns at it.*)

Didn't even say goodbye. Whatever happened to the tradition of old-world courtesy in this country?

(*He puts the 'phone down just as* 'MACBETH' *and* 'LADY MACBETH' *re-enter the room.*)

Who are you, pig-face?

'MACBETH': Landovsky.

INSPECTOR: The actor?

'MACBETH': The floor-cleaner in a boiler factory.

INSPECTOR: That's him. I'm a great admirer of yours, you know. I've followed your career for years.

'MACBETH': I haven't worked for years.

INSPECTOR: What are you talking about?—I saw you last season— my wife was with me . . .

'MACBETH': It couldn't have been me.

INSPECTOR: It *was* you—you looked great—sounded great— where were you last year?

'MACBETH': I was selling papers in—

INSPECTOR: (*Triumphantly*)—the newspaper kiosk at the tram terminus, and you were wonderful! I said to my wife, that's Landovsky—the actor—isn't he great?! What a character! Wonderful voice! "Getcha paper!"—up from here (*He thumps his chest.*)—no strain, every syllable given its value . . . Well, well, well, so now you're sweeping floors, eh? I remember you from way back. I remember you when you were a night-watchman in the builder's yard, and before that when you were the trolley porter at the mortuary, and before *that* when you were the button-moulder in *Peer Gynt* . . . Actually, Pavel, you've had a funny sort of career —it's not my business, of course, but . . . do you know

what you want? It's my opinion that the public is utterly
confused about your intentions. Is this where you saw it all
leading to when you started off so bravely all those years
ago? I remember you in your first job. You were a messenger
—post office, was it . . .?

'MACBETH': *Antony and Cleopatra.*

INSPECTOR: Right!—You see—I'm utterly confused myself. Tell
me Pavel, why did you give it all up?.You were a star! I saw
your Hamlet, your Stanley Kowolski—I saw your Romeo
with what's her name—wonderful girl, whatever happened
to *her*? Oh my God, don't tell me!—could I have your
autograph, it's not for me, it's for my daughter—

'LADY MACBETH': I'd rather not—the last time I signed something
I didn't work for two years.

INSPECTOR: Now, look, don't blame *us* if the parts just stopped
coming. Maybe you got over-exposed.

'LADY MACBETH': I was working in a restaurant at the time.

INSPECTOR: (*Imperturbably*) There you are, you see. The public's
very funny about that sort of thing. They don't want to get
dressed up and arrange a baby-sitter only to find that they've
paid good money to see *Hedda Gabler* done by a waitress.
I'm beginning to understand why your audience is confined
to your circle of acquaintances. (*To audience.*) Don't move.
I mean, it gives one pause, doesn't it? 'Tonight Macbeth
will be played by Mr Landovsky who last season scored a
personal success in the newspaper kiosk at the tram terminus
and has recently been seen washing the floors in number
three boiler factory. The role of Lady Macbeth is in the
capable hands of Vera from The Dirty Spoon' . . . It sounds
like a rough night.

(*The words 'rough night' operate as a cue for the entrance of the*
actor playing MACDUFF.

Enter MACDUFF.)

MACDUFF: O horror, horror, horror!
    Confusion now hath made his masterpiece!

INSPECTOR: What's *your* problem, sunshine? Don't tell me you've
found a corpse—I come here to be taken out of myself, not
to be shown a reflection of the banality of my own life. Why

don't you go out and come in again. I'll get out of the way.
Is this seat taken?

HOSTESS: I'm afraid the performance is not open to the public.

(*Enter* 'ROSS', 'BANQUO', 'MALCOLM', *but not acting*.)

INSPECTOR: I should hope not indeed. That would be acting
without authority—acting without authority!—you'd never
believe I make it up as I go along . . . Right!—sorry to have
interrupted.

(*He sits down. Pause.*)

Any time you're ready.

(*The* HOSTESS *retires. The* ACTORS *remain standing on the
stage, unco-operative, taking their lead from* 'MACBETH'. *The*
INSPECTOR *leaves his seat and approaches* 'MACBETH'.)

INSPECTOR: (*To* 'MACBETH'.) Now listen, you stupid bastard,
you'd better get rid of the idea that there's a special
Macbeth which you do when I'm not around, and some
other *Macbeth* for when I *am* around which isn't worth
doing. You've only got one *Macbeth*. Because I'm giving
this party and there ain't no other. It's what we call a
one-party system. I'm the cream in your coffee, the sugar in
your tank, and the breeze blowing down your neck. So let's
have a little of the old trouper spirit, because if I walk out
of this show I take it with me.

(*He goes back to his seat and says genially to audience.*)
So sorry to interrupt.

(*He sits down.* 'MACBETH' *is still unco-operative.* 'ROSS' *takes
the initiative. He talks quietly to* 'BANQUO', *who leaves to
make his entrance again.* 'LADY MACBETH' *goes behind screen
stage left.*)

    ROSS: Goes the King hence today?

    (*Pause*)

  MACBETH: He does; he did appoint so.

      (*The acting is quick and casual.*)

    ROSS: The night has been unruly.

  MACBETH: 'Twas a rough night.

      (MACDUFF *enters as before.*)

  MACDUFF: O horror, horror, horror!

      Confusion now hath made his masterpiece.

Most sacrilegious murder hath broke ope
The Lord's anointed temple and stole thence
The life of the building.

MACBETH: What is't you say? The life? Mean you His
Majesty?

BANQUO: Ring the alarum bell. Murder and treason.

LADY MACBETH: What's the business,
Speak, speak!

MACDUFF: O gentle lady,
'Tis not for you to hear what I can speak.
(*Alarum bell sounds.*)
Our royal master's murdered.

LADY MACBETH: Woe, alas! What, in our house!

ROSS: Too cruel, anywhere.

MACBETH: (*Enters with bloody daggers.*) Had I but died an
hour before this chance
I had lived a blessed time; far from this instant
There's nothing serious in mortality.
All is but toys; renown and grace is dead,
The wine of life is drawn, and the mere lees
Is left this vault to brag of.
(*Enter* MALCOLM.)

MALCOLM: What is amiss?

MACBETH: You are, and do not know't.

MACDUFF: Your royal father's murdered.

MALCOLM: By whom?

MACBETH: Those of his chamber, as it seemed, had done 't:
Their hands and faces were all badged with
blood:
So were these daggers which unwip't we found
upon their pillows;
Oh yet I do repent me of my fury
That I did kill them.

MALCOLM: Wherefore did you so?

LADY MACBETH: (*Swooning*) Help me hence, ho!

MACBETH: Look to the lady!

MACDUFF: Look to the lady!
(LADY MACBETH *is being taken out.*)

MACBETH: Let us briefly put on manly readiness
         And meet in the hall together.
         (*All, except* MALCOLM *exeunt.*)

MALCOLM: (*Aside*) To show an unfelt sorrow is an office
         Which the false man does easy. I'll to England.
         This murderous shaft that's shot
         Hath not yet lighted; and our safest way
         Is to avoid the aim. Therefore to horse.
         (*Exit.*)

MACDUFF: Malcolm and Donalbain, the King's two sons,
         Are stolen away and fled, which puts upon them
         Suspicion of the deed.

ROSS: Then 'tis most like
      The sovereignty will fall upon Macbeth?

MACDUFF: He is already named and gone to Scone
         To be invested.
         (*Fanfare.*
         They leave the stage. MACBETH *in cloak crowns*
         himself standing above screen.
         The INSPECTOR *applauds and steps forward into the*
         light.)

INSPECTOR: Very good. Very good! And so nice to have a play
with a happy ending for a change.
(*Other* ACTORS *come on-stage in general light.*)
(*To* LADY MACBETH.) Darling, you were marvellous.

'LADY MACBETH': I'm not your darling.

INSPECTOR: I know, and you weren't marvellous either, but when
in Rome *parlezvous* as the natives do. Actually, I thought
you were better on the radio.

'LADY MACBETH': I haven't been on radio.

INSPECTOR: You've been on mine.
(*To the general audience the* INSPECTOR *says.*)
Please don't leave the building. You may use the lavatory
but leave the door open.
(*To* MACBETH.)
Stunning! Incredible! Absolutely fair to middling.

'MACBETH': You were rubbish!

INSPECTOR: Look, just because I didn't laugh out loud it doesn't

mean I wasn't enjoying it. (*To* HOSTESS.) Which one were
you?

HOSTESS: I'm not in it.

INSPECTOR: You're in it, up to here. It's pretty clear to me that
this flat is being used for entertaining men. There is a law
about that, you know.

HOSTESS: I don't think *Macbeth* is what was meant.

INSPECTOR: Who's to say what was meant? Words can be your
friend or your enemy, depending on who's throwing the
book, so watch your language. (*He passes a finger over the
furniture.*) Look at this! Filthy! If this isn't a disorderly
house I've never seen one, and I have seen one. I've had
this place watched you know.

HOSTESS: I know.

INSPECTOR: Gave themselves away, did they?

HOSTESS: It was the uniforms mainly, and standing each side of
the door.

INSPECTOR: My little team. Boris and Maurice.

HOSTESS: One of them examined everyone's papers and the other
one took down the names.

INSPECTOR: Yes, one of them can read and the other one can
write. That's why we go around in threes—I have to keep
an eye on those bloody intellectuals.

'MACDUFF': Look, what the hell do you want?

INSPECTOR: I want to know who's in tonight.

(*He looks at a list of names in his notebook and glances over
the audience.*)

HOSTESS: They are all personal friends of mine.

INSPECTOR: Now let's see who we've got here. (*Looking at the
list.*) Three stokers, two labourers, a van-driver's mate,
janitors, street cleaners, a jobbing gardener, painter and
decorator, chambermaid, two waiters, farmhand. . . . You
seem to have cracked the problem of the working-class
audience. If there isn't a catch I'll put you up as a heroine
of the revolution. I mean, the counter-revolution. No, I tell
a lie, I mean the normalization—Yes, I know. Who is that
horny-handed son of the soil?

(*The* INSPECTOR *points his torch at different people in the audience*.)

HOSTESS: (*Looking into the audience*.) Medieval historian . . . professor of philosophy . . . painter . . .

INSPECTOR: And decorator?

HOSTESS: No . . . lecturer . . . student . . . student . . . defence lawyer . . . Minister of Health in the caretaker government . . .

INSPECTOR: What's he doing now?

HOSTESS: He's a caretaker.

INSPECTOR: Yes, well, I must say a column of tanks is a great leveller. How about the defence lawyer?

HOSTESS: He's sweeping the streets now.

INSPECTOR: You see, some went down, but some went up. Fair do's. Well, I'll tell you what. I don't want to spend all day taking statements. It's frankly not worth the candle for three years' maximum and I know you've been having a run of bad luck all round—jobs lost, children failing exams, letters undelivered, driving licences withdrawn, passports indefinitely postponed—and nothing on paper. It's as if the system had a mind of its own; so why don't you give it a chance, and I'll give you one. I'm really glad I caught you before you closed. If I can make just one tiny criticism . . . Shakespeare—or the Old Bill, as we call him in the force— is not a popular choice with my chief, owing to his popularity with the public, or, as we call it in the force, the filth. The fact is, when you get a universal and timeless writer like Shakespeare, there's a strong feeling that he could be spitting in the eyes of the beholder when he should be keeping his mind on Verona—hanging around the 'gents'. You know what I mean? Unwittingly, of course. He didn't know he was doing it, at least you couldn't prove he did, which is what makes the chief so prejudiced against him. The chief says he'd rather you stood up and said, 'There is no freedom in this country', then there's nothing underhand and we all know where we stand. You get your lads together and we get our lads together and when it's all over, one of us is in power and you're in gaol. That's freedom in action. But what we don't like is a lot of people being cheeky and saying they are only Julius Caesar or Coriolanus or Macbeth.

Otherwise we are going to start treating them the same as the ones who say they are Napoleon. Got it?

'MACBETH': We obey the law and we ask no more of you.

INSPECTOR: The law? I've got the Penal Code tattooed on my whistle, Landovsky, and there's a lot about you in it. Section 98, subversion—anyone acting out of hostility to the state . . . Section 100, incitement—anyone acting out of hostility to the state . . . I could nick you just for acting— and the sentence is double for an organized group, which I can make stick on Robinson Crusoe and his man any day of the week. So don't tell me about the laws.

'MACBETH': We're protected by the Constitution . . .

INSPECTOR: Dear God, and we call you intellectuals. Personally I can't read that stuff. Nobody talks like that so it's not reasonable to expect them to live like it. The way I see it, life is lived off the record. It's altogether too human for the written word, it happens in pictures . . . metaphors . . . A few years ago you suddenly had it on toast, but when they gave you an inch you overplayed your hand and rocked the boat so they pulled the rug from under you, and now you're in the doghouse . . . I mean, that is pure fact. Metaphorically speaking. It describes what happened to you in a way that anybody can understand.

(BANQUO, *henceforth* CAHOOT, *howls like a dog, barks, falls silent on his hands and knees*.)

INSPECTOR: Sit! Here, boy! What's his name?

'MACBETH': Cahoot.

INSPECTOR: The social parasite and slanderer of the state?

CAHOOT: The writer.

INSPECTOR: That's him. You're a great favourite down at the nick, you know. We're thinking of making you writer in residence for a couple of years; four if you're a member of a recognized school, which I can make stick on a chimpanzee with a box of alphabet bricks. (*Smiles*) Would you care to make a statement?

CAHOOT: 'Thou hast it now: King, Cawdor, Glamis, all
    As the weird sisters promised . . .'

INSPECTOR: Kindly leave my wife's family out of this.

CAHOOT: '. . . and I fear
> thou playedst most foully for't . . .'

INSPECTOR: Foul . . . fair . . . which is which? That's two witches:
one more and we can do the show right here.

CAHOOT: '. . . Yet it was said
> It should not stand in thy posterity . . .'

INSPECTOR: If you think you can drive a horse and cart through
the law of slander by quoting blank verse at me, Cahoot,
you're going to run up against what we call poetic justice:
which means we get you into line if we have to chop one of
your feet off. You know as well as I do that this performance
of yours goes right against the spirit of normalization. When
you clean out the stables, Cahoot, the muck is supposed to
go into the gutter, not find its way back into the stalls. (*To*
ALL *generally.*) I blame sport and religion for all this, you
know. An Olympic games here, a papal visit there, and
suddenly you think you can take liberties with your freedom
. . . amateur theatricals, organized groups, committees of all
kinds—listen, I've arrested more committees (*to* 'BANQUO')
than you've had dog's dinners. I arrested the Committee to
Defend the Unjustly Persecuted for saying I unjustly
persecuted the Committee for Free Expression, which I
arrested for saying there wasn't any—so if I find that this
is a benefit for the Canine Defence League you're going to
feel my hand on your collar and I don't care if Moscow
Dynamo is at home to the Vatican in the European Cup.
('BANQUO' *growls.*)
What is the matter with him?

'MACBETH': He's been made a non-person.

INSPECTOR: Has he? Well, between you and me and these three
walls and especially the ceiling, barking up the wrong tree
comes under anti-state agitation. I'm not having him fouling
the system let alone the pavements just because he's got an
identity crisis.

'MACBETH': Your system could do with a few antibodies. If
you're afraid to risk the infection of an uncontrolled idea,
the first time a new one gets in, it'll run through your
system like a rogue bacillus. Remember the last time.

INSPECTOR: (*Pause.*) Yes. Well, a lot of water has passed through
the Penal Code since then. Things are normalizing nicely. I
expect this place will be back to normal in five minutes . . .
Eh? Nice Dog! Well, I wonder what the weather's like
outside . . . (*Moves*) Please leave in an orderly manner, and
don't cheek the policeman on the way out.
(*'Phone rings. He picks it up . . . listens, replaces it.*)
Cloudy, with a hint of rain.
(*He exits.*
*He leaves. The police car is heard to depart with its siren
going.*)

CAHOOT: Let it come down!
(*The performance continues from Act Three Scene
One. All exeunt except* CAHOOT.)

BANQUO: Thou has it now: King, Cawdor, Glamis, all
As the weird women promised; and I fear
Thou playdst most foully for't. Yet it was said
It should not stand in thy posterity
But that myself should be the root and father
Of many kings. If there come truth from them,
As upon thee, Macbeth, their speeches shine,
Why by the verities on thee made good
(MACBETH *enters.*)
May they not be my oracles as well
And set me up in hope? But hush! No more.

MACBETH: Tonight we hold a solemn supper, sir,
And I'll request your presence.
Ride you this afternoon?

BANQUO: Ay, my good lord.

MACBETH: Fail not our feast.

BANQUO: My lord, I will not.
(*Exit* BANQUO.)

MACBETH: Our fears in Banquo
Stick deep; and in his royalty of nature
Reigns that which would be feared. He chid the
sisters
When first they put the name of king upon me,
And bade them speak to him. Then, prophet-like

            They hailed him father to a line of kings.
            Upon my head they placed a fruitless crown
            And put a barren sceptre in my grip,
            Thence to be wrenched with an unlineal hand,
            No son of mine succeeding. If it be so,
            For Banquo's issue have I filed my mind,
            For them the gracious Duncan have I murdered.
            Rather than so, come, fate, into the list
            And champion me to the utterance!
            (MACBETH *moves screen to reveal two* MURDERERS.)
            Was it not yesterday we spoke together?
            (*Lights down.*)

1ST MURDERER: It was, so please your highness.

MACBETH: Well then now,
            Have you considered of my speeches? Know
            That it was he in the times past which held you
            So under fortune, which you thought had been
            Our innocent self.

1ST MURDERER: You made it known to us.

MACBETH: I did so. Are you so gospelled,
            To pray for this good man and for his issue,
            Whose heavy hand hath bowed you to the grave,
            And beggared yours for ever?

2ND MURDERER: I am one, my liege,
            Whom the vile blows and buffets of the world
            Hath so incensed that I am reckless what I do
            To spite the world.

1ST MURDERER: And I another,
            So weary with disasters, tugged with fortune,
            That I would set my life on any chance
            To mend it or be rid on't.

MACBETH: Both of you
            Know Banquo was your enemy.

MURDERERS: True, my lord.

MACBETH: So is he mine, and though I could
            With bare-faced power sweep him from my sight
            And bid my will avouch it, yet I must not.

2ND MURDERER: We shall, my lord

Perform what you command us.

IST MURDERER: We are resolved, my lord.

(EASY's *lorry has been heard to draw up outside.
The* MURDERERS *go to the window and open
shutters.* MACBETH *leaves saying.*)

MACBETH: (*Aside*) It is concluded! Banquo, thy soul's flight,
If it find heaven, must find it out tonight.
(*The* MURDERERS *take up position to ambush*
BANQUO. EASY *appears at window and says.*)

EASY: Buxtons . . . Almost Leamington Spa.
(*The* MURDERERS *are surprised to see him.* EASY
*disappears from window: they peer outside to see
him, but meanwhile* EASY *has entered room.*)
Cakehops.

IST MURDERER: But who did bid thee join with us?

EASY: Buxtons.

(*Pause*)

2ND MURDERER: (*With misgiving.*) He needs not our mistrust,
since he delivers
Our offices and what we have to do
To the direction just.

EASY: Eh?

IST MURDERER: Then stand with us;
The west yet glimmers with some streaks of day.
Now spurs the lated traveller apace
To gain the timely inn; and near approaches
The subject of our watch.

(*Pause*)

EASY: Eh?

BANQUO: (*Off-stage*) Give us a light, here, ho!

2ND MURDERER: Then 'tis he.

(*Enter* BANQUO *in window.*)

IST MURDERER: Stand to 't!

BANQUO: It will be rain tonight.

IST MURDERER: Let it come down!

(*The two* MURDERERS *attack* BANQUO.)

BANQUO: O treachery!

(*He flees off-stage with the two* MURDERERS *in*

pursuit. EASY *remains, looking bewildered. The*
HOSTESS *appears from the audience again.*)

EASY: Buxtons . . . cake hops . . . almost Leamington
 Spa . . .
 (*The* HOSTESS *leads him off-stage. Light and music*
 for MACBETH'S *feast.* MACBETH *enters with* LADY
 MACBETH *and guests in attendance.*)

MACBETH: You know your own degrees, sit down.
 At first and last a hearty welcome.

GUESTS: Thanks to your majesty.

MACBETH: Ourself will mingle with society
 And play the humble host.
 (*The* GUESTS *have brought their own stools and*
 goblets. LADY MACBETH *enters likewise.* IST
 MURDERER *enters with* EASY, *remaining at the edge*
 of the stage.)
 Be large in mirth. Anon we'll drink a measure
 The table round.
 (*He sees* IST MURDERER *and goes to him.*)
 There's blood upon thy face!

IST MURDERER: 'Tis Banquo's then.

MACBETH: Is he dispatched?

IST MURDERER: My lord, his throat is cut;
 That I did for him.

MACBETH: Thanks for that.
 Get thee gone! Tomorrow we will hear ourselves
 again.
 (*Exit* MURDERER, *followed by* EASY. *During the*
 scene EASY *is hovering at the fringes, hoping to*
 catch someone's eye. His entrances and exits
 coincide with those for BANQUO'S GHOST, *who is*
 invisible, and he only appears in MACBETH'S
 eyeline. MACBETH *does his best to ignore him.*)

LADY MACBETH: My royal lord,
 You do not give the cheer.

MACBETH: Sweet remembrancer!
 Now good digestion wait on appetite,
 And health on both!

ROSS: May't please your highness sit.

MACBETH: Here had we now our country's honour roofed,
Were the graced person of our Banquo present.

ROSS: His absence, sir,
Lays blame upon his promise. Please't your
highness
To grace us with your royal company?
Here is a place reserved.
(EASY *enters at door stage right.*)

MACBETH: Where?

ROSS: Here, my good lord. What is't that moves your
highness?

MACBETH: Which of you have done this?

ROSS: What, my good lord?

MACBETH: Thou canst not say I did it; never shake
Thy gory locks at me.

ROSS: Gentlemen, rise. His highness is not well.

LADY MACBETH: Sit, worthy friends. My lord is often thus;
The fit is momentary; upon a thought
He will again be well.
(*She crosses to* MACBETH.)
Are you a man?

MACBETH: Ay, and a bold one, that dare look on that
Which might appall the devil.

LADY MACBETH: O proper stuff!
Why do you make such faces? When all's done
You look but on a stool.
(EASY *appears at window.*)

MACBETH: Prithee, see there!
Behold! Look! Lo!
(*He points, but* EASY *has lost his nerve, and
disappears just as she turns round.*)

LADY MACBETH: What, quite unmanned in folly?

MACBETH: If I stand here, I saw him. This is more strange
Than such a murder is.

LADY MACBETH: My worthy lord,
Your noble friends do lack you.

MACBETH: I do forget.

(*He recovers somewhat.*)

Do not muse at me, my most worthy friends:
I have a strange infirmity, which is nothing
To those that know me. Come love and health to
   all!
Then I'll sit down. Give me some wine; Fill full!
I drink to the general joy o' the whole table,
And to our dear friend Banquo, whom we miss.
Would he were here! To all—and him—we thirst,
And all to all.

GUESTS: Our duties and the pledge!

(*However,* EASY *tries again, reappearing in*
MACBETH's *sight above screen stage right.*)

MACBETH: Avaunt, and quit my sight!

(EASY *quits his sight.*)

Let the earth hide thee!
Thy bones are marrowless, thy blood is cold.

LADY MACBETH: Think of this, good peers,
But as a thing of custom; 'tis no other;
Only it spoils the pleasure of the time.

(EASY *appears at the window again.*)

MACBETH: Hence, horrible shadow!
Unreal mockery, hence!

(*He closes shutters. He recovers again.*)

Why, so; being gone,
I am a man again. Pray you sit still.

LADY MACBETH: (*Aside to* MACBETH.) You have displaced the
   mirth, broke the good meeting
With most admired disorder.

(*To the* GUESTS.) At once, good night.
Stand not upon the order of your going;
But go at once.

(*The* GUESTS *rise and depart.*)

ROSS: Good night; and better health
Attend his majesty!

LADY MACBETH: A kind good-night to all!

(*Lights down.*)

MACBETH: It will have blood, they say; blood will have blood.

Stones have been known to move and trees to
    speak;
And betimes I will—to the weird sisters.
More shall they speak; for now I am bent to
    know
By the worst means the worst.
(*Thunder and lightning. Three* WITCHES.)

WITCHES: Double, double, toil and trouble;
Fire burn, and cauldron bubble.

1ST WITCH: By the pricking of my thumbs,
Something wicked this way comes.
(*Enter* MACBETH.)

MACBETH: How now, you secret, black, and midnight hags!
What is't you do?

WITCHES: A deed without a name.

MACBETH: I conjure you, by that which you profess,
Howe'er you come to know it, answer me—

1ST WITCH: Say if thou'dst rather hear it from our mouths
Or from our masters.

MACBETH: Call 'em. Let me see 'em.
(*The 'Apparitions' of Shakespeare's play are here
translated into voices, amplified and coming from
different parts of the auditorium. Evidently*
MACBETH *can see the 'Apparition' from which
each voice comes. Thunder.*)

1ST VOICE: Macbeth, Macbeth, Macbeth, beware Macduff!
Beware the Thane of Fife! Dismiss me. Enough.

MACBETH: Whate'er thou art, for thy good caution, thanks;
Thou hast harped my fear aright.

2ND VOICE: Macbeth, Macbeth, Macbeth!

MACBETH: Had I three ears, I'd hear thee.

2ND VOICE: Be bloody, bold, and resolute; laugh to scorn
The power of man; for none of woman born
Shall harm Macbeth.

MACBETH: Then live Macduff; What need I fear of thee?
(*Thunder.*
Exit WITCHES.)
What is this

That rises like the issue of a king,
And wears upon his baby brow the round
And top of a sovereignty?

CHILD'S VOICE: Be lion-mettled, proud, and take no care
Who chafes, who frets, or where conspirers are;
Macbeth shall never vanquished be, until
Great Birnam Wood to high Dunsinane Hill
Shall come against him.

MACBETH: That will never be.
Who can impress the forest, bid the tree
Unfix his earth-bound root? Yet my heart
Throbs to know one thing:

WITCHES: (*Off-stage*) Seek to know no more.
Show his eyes and grieve his heart;
Come like shadows, so depart.

MACBETH: Where are they? Gone! Let this pernicious hour
Stand aye accursed in the calendar.
Come in, without there.
(*Enter* LENNOX.)

LENNOX: What is your grace's will.

MACBETH: Saw you the weird sisters?

LENNOX: No my lord.
(EASY *passes window.*)

MACBETH: Who was't come by?

LENNOX: 'Tis two or three my lord, that bring you word
that
Macduff's fled to England.

MACBETH: Fled to England?
(EASY *enters timidly.*)

EASY: Useless . . . useless . . . Buxtons cake hops . . . artichoke
almost Leamington Spa . . . [* Afternoon . . . afternoon . . .
Buxtons blocks and that . . . lorry from Leamington Spa.]

'MACBETH': What?
(*General light.* OTHERS, *but not* MALCOLM *or* MACDUFF,
approach out of curiosity. 'MACBETH' *says to* HOSTESS.)
Who the hell is this man?

HOSTESS: (*To* EASY.) Who are you?
(EASY *has his clipboard which he offers.*)

EASY: Buxton cake hops.

HOSTESS: Don't sign anything.

EASY: Blankets up middling if season stuck, after plug-holes kettle-drummed lightly A412 mildly Rickmansworth— clipped awful this water ice, zig-zaggled—splash quarterly trainers as Micky Mouse snuffle—cup—evidently knick-knacks quarantine only if bacteriologic waistcoats crumble pipe—sniffle then postbox but shazam!!!! Even platforms— dandy avuncular Donald Duck never-the-less minty magazines! [*Translation—see page 20]

(*Pause*)

'MACBETH': Eh?

(EASY *produces a phrase book and starts thumbing through it.*)

EASY: (*Triumphantly*) Ah!

(*He passes the* HOSTESS *his phrase book, indicating what she should read. She examines the page.*)

HOSTESS: He says his postillion has been struck by lightning.

EASY: Hat rack timble cuckoo pig exit dunce!

'MACBETH': What?

EASY: Dunce!

'MACBETH': What?

EASY: Cuckoo pig exit what.

(*Nodding agreeably.*) Cake hops properly Buxtons.

(*The* HOSTESS *flips through the book.*)

HOSTESS: Cake hops.

EASY: Cake hops.

HOSTESS: Timber or wood.

EASY: Timber or wood—properly Buxtons.

HOSTESS: I'm so sorry about this . . .

EASY: Right. Timber or wood—properly Buxtons. I'm so sorry about this.

(*He opens shutters to reveal his lorry.*)

Ankle so artichoke—almost Leamington Spa.

LENNOX: Oh. He's got a lorry out there.

HOSTESS: Lorry load of wood or timber.

EASY: I'm so sorry about this.

HOSTESS: Don't apologize.

EASY: Don't apologize.

LENNOX: Oh, you do speak the language!

EASY: Oh, you do speak the language.

'MACBETH': No—we speak the language!

EASY: We speak the language.

LENNOX: Cretin is he?

EASY: Pan-stick-trog.

> (*Everybody leaves.*
> *Enter* MALCOLM AND MACDUFF.)

MALCOLM: Let us seek out some desolate shade, and there
Weep our sad bosoms empty.

MACDUFF: Let us rather
Hold fast the mortal sword; and like good men
Bestride our down-fallen birthdom. Each new
morn
New widows howl, new orphans cry, new sorrows
Strike heaven on the face, that it resounds
As if it felt with Scotland, and yelled out
Like syllable of dolour.

MALCOLM: This tyrant, whose sole name blisters our tongues,
Was once thought honest.

MACDUFF: Bleed, bleed, poor country!
(*Police siren is heard in distance.*)

MALCOLM: It weeps, it bleeds, and each new day a gash
Is added to her wounds.

MACDUFF: O Scotland, Scotland!
O nation miserable,
With an untitled tyrant, bloody-sceptred,
When shalt thou see thy wholesome days again.
See who comes here.
(*Siren stops.*)

MALCOLM: My countryman; but yet I know him not.
(*The police car has been wailing on its way back.*
INSPECTOR *enters.*)

MACDUFF: Stands Scotland where it did?

INSPECTOR: Och aye, it's a braw bricht moonlicht nicked, and so
are you, you haggis-headed dumbwits, hoots mon ye must
think I was born yesterday. (*He drops the accent: to the
audience*)—Stay where you are and nobody use the lavatory...

(CAHOOT *enters*.)

Cahoots mon! Where's McLandovsky got himself?

(EASY *enters*. HOSTESS *follows*.)

EASY: Useless, git . . . [*Afternoon, sir . . .]

INSPECTOR: Who are you, pig-face?

(INSPECTOR *grabs him*. EASY *yelps and looks at his watch*.)

EASY: Poxy queen! [*Twenty past ouch.]

Marzipan clocks! [*Watch it!]

INSPECTOR: What?

HOSTESS: He doesn't understand you.

INSPECTOR: What's that language he's talking?

HOSTESS: At the moment we're not sure if it's a language or a clinical condition.

EASY: (*Aggrieved*) Quinces carparks! (*Offering the clipboard*.) Cake-hops—Buxton's almost Leamington Spa.

HOSTESS: He's delivering wood and wants someone to sign for it.

EASY: . . . wood and wants someone to sign for it.

INSPECTOR: Wood?

HOSTESS: He's got a two-ton artichoke out there.

INSPECTOR: What???

HOSTESS: I mean a lorry.

(CAHOOT *taps* EASY *on shoulder*.)

CAHOOT: Useless . . . [*Afternoon . . .]

EASY: (*Absently*) Useless . . . (*then sees who it is*.) *Cahoot*! Geraniums!? [*How are you!?]

CAHOOT: Gymshoes. Geraniums? [*Fine. How are you?]

EASY: Gymshoes.

CAHOOT: Upside cakeshops? (*Have you brought the blocks?]

EASY: Slab. [*Yes.]

CAHOOT: Almost Leamington Spa? [*From Leamington Spa?]

EASY: Slab, git. Even artichoke. [*Yes, sir. I've got a lorry.]

CAHOOT: Cube. [*Thanks.]

(*He signs clipboard*.)

EASY: Cube, git. [*Thank you, sir.]

INSPECTOR: Just a minute. What the hell are you talking about?

CAHOOT: Afternoon, squire!

INSPECTOR: Afternoon. Who's your friend?

HOSTESS: He's the cake-hops man.

INSPECTOR: Well, why can't he say so?

CAHOOT: He only speaks Dogg.

INSPECTOR: What?

CAHOOT: Dogg.

INSPECTOR: Dogg?

CAHOOT: Haven't you heard of it?

INSPECTOR: Where did you learn it?

CAHOOT: You don't learn it, you catch it.

    (EASY *notices* 'MALCOLM'.)

EASY: Useless. [*Afternoon.]

'MALCOLM': Useless . . . Geraniums?

EASY: Gymshoes. Geraniums?

'MALCOLM': Gymshoes . . . cube . . .

EASY: (*To* CAHOOT.) Blankets up middling if senses stuck, after
    plug-holes kettle-drummed lightly A412 mildly
    Rickmansworth.

'MALCOLM': Rickmansworth.

'MACDUFF': (*To* 'MALCOLM', *heading for the door*.) He needs a bit
    of a hand . . .

EASY: Slab.

'MALCOLM': (*Leaving*.) . . . with the cake-hops . . .

EASY: Clipped awful this water ice zig-zaggled.

CAHOOT: His mate got struck down by lightning.

HOSTESS: Shazam . . .

EASY: Slab.

CAHOOT: (*Hands* EASY *the plans*.) Albatross. [*Plans.]
    (*To* EASY.) Easy! Brick . . .

EASY: Slab, git.

CAHOOT: Brick. (*He positions* EASY *for building steps*.)

EASY: Brick? [*Here?]

CAHOOT: Cake-hops. Brick.

EASY: Cube, git. [*Thanks, sir.]

CAHOOT/HOSTESS: Gymshoes. [*Excellent.]

INSPECTOR: May I remind you we're supposed to be in a period
    of normalization here.

HOSTESS: Kindly leave the stage. Act Five is about to begin.

INSPECTOR: Is it! I must warn you that anything you say will be
    taken down and played back at your trial.

HOSTESS: Bicycles! Plank? [*Ready?]
    (*To* INSPECTOR.) Slab. Gymshoes!
    (CAHOOT *and* HOSTESS *leave.*
    INSPECTOR *and* EASY *are left.*)

INSPECTOR: What gymshoes?

EASY: What, git? [*Eleven, sir?]

INSPECTOR: Gymshoes!

EASY: Slab, git.

INSPECTOR: (*Giving up.*) Useless . . .

EASY: (*Enthusiastically*) Useless, git! [*Afternoon, sir!]

INSPECTOR: Right—that's it! (*To ceiling.*) Roger! (*To the audience.*)
    Put your hands on your heads. Put your—placay manos—
    per capita . . . nix toiletto!
    (*'Phone rings.* EASY *answers, hands it to* INSPECTOR.)

EASY: Roger.

INSPECTOR: (*Into 'phone.*) Did you get all that? Clear as a what?
    Acting out of hostility to the Republic. Ten years minimum.
    I want every word in evidence.
    (LADY MACBETH *enters with lighted taper.*)

LADY MACBETH: Hat, daisy puck! Hat, so fie! Sun, dock: hoops
           malign my cattlegrid! Smallish peacocks!
           Flaming scots git, flaming! Fireplace nought
           jammy-flits?
    (*'Phone rings.* INSPECTOR *picks it up.*)

INSPECTOR: (*Into 'phone: pause.*) How the hell do I know? But if
    it's not free expression, I don't know what is!
    (*Hangs up.*)

LADY MACBETH: (*Dry-washing her hands.*) Ash-loving pell-mell on.
           Fairly buses gone Arabia nettle-rash old icicles
             nun. Oh oh oh . . .
           [*Here's the smell of the blood still. All the
             perfumes of Arabia will not sweeten this little
             hand . . .]
           (*She exits.*)

INSPECTOR: (*To* EASY.) She's making it up as she goes along.
    You must think I'm—
    (*But* EASY *is glowing with the light of recognition.*)

EASY: . . . Ah . . . *Macbeth!*

(*Sound of cannon. Smoke.* MACBETH, *armed, appears on battlement.*)

MACBETH: Sack-cloth never pullovers!—wickets to flicks.
Such Birnam cakeshops carousals Dunisnane!
. . . Dovetails oboes Malcolm? Crossly window-
framed!
[*Bring me no more reports. Let them fly all
Till Birnam Wood remove to Dunsinane.
What's the boy Malcolm? Was he not born of
woman?]

('*Phone rings.* INSPECTOR *snatches it.*)

INSPECTOR: (*Into 'phone.*) What? No—crossly window-framed, I
think . . . Hang about—

MACBETH: Fetlocked his trade-offs cried terrain!
Pram Birnam cakehops bolsters Dunisnane!
[*I will not be afraid of death and bane
Till Birnam Forest come to Dunsinane!]

(*The back of the lorry opens, revealing* MALCOLM *and* OTHERS
within, unloading the blocks etc. INSPECTOR *sees this—speaks
into walkie-talkie.*)

INSPECTOR: Get the chief. Get the chief!

(*One or two—*ROSS, LENNOX—*are to get off the lorry to form a
human chain for the blocks and slabs etc. to pass from
MACDUFF in the lorry to EASY building the steps.*)

MALCOLM: (*To* MACDUFF *who is in the lorry with him.*)
Jugged cake-hops furnished soon? [*What wood
is this before us?]

INSPECTOR: (*Into walkie-talkie.*) Wilco zebra over!

MACDUFF: Sin cake-hops Birnam, git. [*The woods of
Birnam, sir.]

INSPECTOR: Green Charlie Angels 15 out.

MALCOLM: State level filberts blacken up aglow . . . [*Let
every soldier hew him down a bough . . .]

INSPECTOR: Easy Dogg!

EASY: (*To* INSPECTOR.) Slab, git?

MALCOM: Fry lettuce denial! [*And bear it before him!]

(MACDUFF *and* ANOTHER *leap off lorry; blocks start flowing
towards* EASY, *who builds steps.*

LADY MACBETH—*Wails and crys off-stage.*
MESSENGER *enters.*)

MESSENGER: Git! Margarine distract! [*The queen, my lord
             is dead!]

MACBETH: Dominoes, et dominoes, et dominoes,
           Popsies historical axle-grease, exacts bubbly fins
             crock lavender . . .
           [*Tomorrow, and tomorrow, and tomorrow,
           Creeps in this petty pace from day to day to the
             last syllable of recorded time . . .]

INSPECTOR: (*Into 'phone.*) Yes, chief! I think everything's more or
less under control chief . . .
(*This is a lie. The steps are building,* MACBETH *is continuing his
soliloquy, in Dogg: drums and cannons . . . and—*)

MACDUFF: Docket tanks, tarantaras!
           [*Make all our trumpets speak!]

(*Trumpets sound.*
And a MESSENGER *rushes in for* MACBETH.)

MESSENGER: Flummoxed git! [*Gracious lord!]

MACBETH: Docket! [*Speak!]

MESSENGER: Cenotaph pay Birnam fry prevailing
             cakehops voluntary!
           [*As I did stand my watch upon the hill
           I looked toward Birnam and anon methought
           The wood began to move.]

MACBETH: Quinces icepacks! [*Liar and slave!]

(MESSENGER *retreats.*)

(*Throughout the above,* EASY *is calling for, and receiving, in the
right order, four planks, three slabs, five blocks and nine cubes;
unwittingly using the English words.*
Meanwhile, MACDUFF *has confronted* MACBETH.)

MACDUFF: Spiral, tricycle, spiral! [*Turn, hellhound, turn!]

MACBETH: Rafters Birnam cakehops hobble Dunsinane,
           fry counterpane nit crossly window-framed,
           fancifully oblong! Sundry cobbles
           rattling up so chamberlain. Frantic, Macduff!
           Fry butter ban loss underlay—November glove!
           [*Though Birnam Wood be come to Dunsinane

> And thou opposed, being of no woman born,
> Yet will I try the last. Before my body
> I throw my warlike shield. Lay on, Macduff;
> and damned be him that first cries 'Hold
> enough!']

INSPECTOR: (*Interrupts.*) All right! That's it!

(*The* INSPECTOR *mounts the now completed platform.*)

INSPECTOR: Thank you. Thank you! Thank you! Scabs!
Stinking slobs—crooks. You're nicked, Jock.
Punks make me puke. Kick back, I'll break necks,
smack chops, put yobs in padlocks and fix facts.
Clamp down on poncy gits like a ton of bricks.

(CAHOOT *applauds.*)

CAHOOT: Gymshoes. Marmalade. Yob?

(*General applause.*)

EASY: Yobbo, git.

INSPECTOR: Boris! Maurice!

(*Two* POLICEMEN *enter and stand to receive slabs thrown to them from the doorway.*)

MACDUFF: Spiral, tricycle, spiral!

INSPECTOR: Slab!

(*Grey slabs are now thrown in and caught by* BORIS *and* MAURICE *who build a wall across the proscenium opening as* MACBETH *and* MACDUFF *fight and* MACBETH *is slain. 'Phone rings.* EASY *picks it up.*)

EASY: Oh, useless gettie!

(*While* EASY *speaks into the 'phone, the* INSPECTOR *directs the building of the wall with the help of* BORIS *and* MAURICE, *the policemen; and* MALCOLM *mounts the platform, taking the crown off the dead* MACBETH, *and finally placing it on his own head.*)

MALCOLM: Nit laughable a cretin awful pig.

EASY: Cretinous fascist pig like one o'clock. Slab?

MALCOLM: Prefer availing avaricious moorhens et factotum after.

EASY: Rozzers. Gendarmes—filth!

MALCOLM: Centre roundabout if partly lawnmowers rosebush.

EASY: Blockhead. Brick as too planks. Slab.

MALCOLM: Gracious laxative. [*Dead butcher.]

EASY: Fishes bastard. Kick his backside so help me Dogg. See if I
    don't. Normalization.

MALCOLM: Vivay hysterical nose poultice.

EASY: Double double toil and trouble.

MALCOLM: Alabaster ominous nifty, blanket noon
           Howl cinder trellis pistols owl by Scone.
           [* So, thanks to all at once and to each one,
           Whom we invite to see us crowned at Scone.]

    (*Fanfare*)

EASY: (*Over fanfare.*) Double double. Double double toil and
    trouble. No. Shakespeare.

    (*Silence*)

    Well, it's been a funny sort of week. But I should be back
    by Tuesday.

ff

Contemporary Classics

'Faber is well known for its drama output, but its new series of collected plays, *Contemporary Classics*, is particularly worth owning because of both the content and the chic look of the books. Featured authors represent a who's who of contemporary theatre and all are primarily masters of the verbal art. *Highly recommended*.' Steve Grant, **Time Out**

Alan Ayckbourn: Plays One
Alan Bennett: Plays One
Steven Berkoff:
Plays One and Plays Two
Brian Friel: Plays One
Trevor Griffiths: Plays One
Christopher Hampton: Plays One
David Hare:
Plays One and Plays Two
Tony Harrison: Plays Three
Ronald Harwood: Plays Two
Sharman Macdonald: Plays One
Frank McGuinness: Plays One
John Osborne: Plays One
Harold Pinter:
Plays One, Plays Two, Plays Three and Plays Four
Sam Shepard: Plays Two
Wallace Shawn: Plays One
Tom Stoppard:
Plays One and Plays Two
Nick Ward: Plays One
Timberlake Wertenbaker: Plays One

ORDER FORM

Purchase these books in your local bookshop,
or order them direct from us.

Please send me:

____	Alan Ayckbourn: Plays One (0 571 17680 1)	£8.99
____	Alan Bennett: Plays One (0 571 17745 X)	£9.99
____	Steven Berkoff: Plays One (0 571 16903 1)	£8.99
____	Steven Berkoff: Plays Two (0 571 17102 8)	£8.99
____	Brian Friel: Plays One (0 571 17767 0)	£9.99
____	Trevor Griffiths: Plays One (0 571 17742 5)	£8.99
____	Christopher Hampton: Plays One (0 571 17834 0)	£9.99
____	David Hare: Plays One (0 571 17741 7)	£8.99
____	David Hare: Plays Two (0 571 17835 9)	£9.99
____	Tony Harrison: Plays Three (0 571 19966 5)	£8.99
____	Ronald Harwood: Plays Two (0 571 17401 9)	£9.99
____	Sharman Macdonald: Plays One (0 571 17621 6)	£8.99
____	Frank McGuinness: Plays One (0 571 17740 9)	£8.99
____	John Osborne: Plays One (0 571 17766 2)	£8.99
____	Harold Pinter: Plays One (0 571 17844 8)	£8.99
____	Harold Pinter: Plays Two (0 571 17744 1)	£9.99
____	Harold Pinter: Plays Three (0 571 17845 6)	£8.99
____	Harold Pinter: Plays Four (0 571 17850 2)	£8.99
____	Sam Shepard: Plays Two (0 571 19074 X)	£8.99
____	Wallace Shawn: Plays One (0 571 19092 8)	£9.99
____	Tom Stoppard: Plays One (0 571 17765 4)	£9.99
____	Tom Stoppard: Plays Two (0 571 19008 1)	£8.99
____	Nick Ward: Plays One (0 571 17681 X)	£8.99
____	Timberlake Wertenbaker: Plays One (0 571 17743 3)	£8.99

Total including free postage and packing   £ _____

I enclose a cheque for £ _____ made payable to Faber and Faber Ltd.

Please charge my: Access   Visa   Amex   Diner's Club   Eurocard

Cardholder _____   Expiry Date _____

Account No _____ _____ Name _____

Address _____

Signed _____   Date _____

Send to:
Faber Book Services, Burnt Mill, Elizabeth Way, Harlow, Essex CM20 2HX
Tel 01279 417134 Fax 01279 417366

3318